D0627945

To Marianna

Soutine

A POEM

*"There are
no lines
in nature!"*

BY
Rick Mullin

Enjoy
~~Rudy~~
Rick

DOS MADRES

2012

DOS MADRES PRESS INC.

P.O.Box 294, Loveland, Ohio 45140

www.dosmadres.com   editor@dosmadres.com

Dos Madres is dedicated to the belief that the small press is essential
to the vitality of contemporary literature as a carrier of the new voice,
as well as the older, sometimes forgotten voices of the past. And in an
ever more virtual world, to the creation of fine books pleasing to the
eye and hand.

Dos Madres is named in honor of Vera Murphy and Libbie Hughes,
the "Dos Madres" whose contributions have made this press possible.

Dos Madres Press, Inc. is an Ohio Not For Profit Corporation and a
501 (c) (3) qualified public charity. Contributions are tax deductible.

Executive Editor: Robert J. Murphy

Illustration & Book Design: Elizabeth H. Murphy
www.illusionstudios.net
Typset in Adobe Garamond Pro, FZ Hand 28
Library of Congress Control Number: 2011943016
ISBN 978-1-933675-68-8

Paintings used in Illustration:
Front Cover:
Chaïm Soutine, French, 1893 – 1943 *Self Portrait*, ca. 1918
Oil on canvas, 54.6 x 45.7 cm.(21 ½ x 18 in.)
The Henry and Rose Pearlman Foundation; on long-term loan to
Princeton University Art Museum. (L.1988.62.23)
Photo: Bruce M. White
Back Cover:
Rick Mullin, *Self Portrait*, 2007, Oil on canvas, 14 x 11 in.

ACKNOWLEDGEMENTS

Sections of *Soutine* have appeared in print and online journals, including *The Raintown Review* (Book II, Chapter 4, part I), *The Red Wheel Barrow Poets IV* (Book II, Chapter 2), *American Arts Quarterly*–online, (Book IV, Chapter 2, parts II and III), *Local Knowledge* (Book I, Chapter 2; Book IV, Chapter 1), and *The Nervous Breakdown* (Book I, Chapter 1). I would like to thank the editors of these publications for their support.

I owe much to Marybeth Rua-Larsen and Cally Conan-Davies for their critique of my manuscript and for their encouragement. I would also like to thank the poets Wendy Sloan, Eric Thomas Norris, Mike Alexander, Claudia Serea, Bill Carpenter, and R. Nemo Hill for their insights on chapters of *Soutine*. Thanks to Donald Zirilli for a research lead in Book V. Thanks to all at the Eratoshpere online poetry workshop. And special thanks to my excellent editor, Michele Arboit.

I owe much to Paul Weingarten whose pleasure in reading the final draft of *Soutine* mattered enormously, and to Andrey Tamarchenko for establishing a presence essential to the story. Thanks to both for their friendship.

Special thanks to Meredith Bergmann and David Mason.

Thanks to Elizabeth and Robert Murphy of Dos Madres Press for their confidence in this poem, their effort at producing a beautiful book, and their commitment to publishing poetry.

Thanks always to my wife, Maureen, and to my daughters, Emily, Marguerite, and Lydia, for their generosity and love.

Soutine is dedicated to the memory of Chaïm Soutine.

Rick Mullin

Here the mystery of the greatest painting shines forth, flesh more like flesh than flesh itself, nerves more like nerves than nerves, even if they are painted with streams of rubies, with sulfur on fire, droplets of turquoise, emerald lakes crushed with sapphires, streaks of purple and pearl, a palpitation of silver that quivers and shines, a wondrous flame that wrings matter to its depths after having smelted all the jewels of its mines.
—Elie Faure

This painter of genius came from a society in which there was not simply no background of painting but a positive hostility to painting, so that painting for him was not just a luxury but a forbidden fruit.
—David Sylvester

table of contents

BOOK V

EPILOGUE

AFTERWORD

Book
I

Chapter 1

Portrait of the Village Idiot

I

A charcoal line divides the wrinkled scrap
of butcher's rag. And in a lightning strike,
another follows. A child's fingers snap

and fumble with a brittle charcoal spike.
It crumbles, leaving marks that coalesce
into an aquiline and golem-like

portrayal. Repeatedly the fingers press
the black material into the brown—
a beard, the eyes, an overcoat. A mess.

They tear the paper. And they throw it down
as charcoal limns a landscape in the sky
and February hunkers over town.

II

And blood will fall. A life of Chaïm Soutine
would almost have to drip in lacquered red
across a crusted base of brown and green.

In the beginning? Well, the rabbi's head.
The nightmares that transgression might engender,
and the power of nature. Elemental dread

as, liver-lipped, the tenth child of the mender
waddles through the gray-slate thaw of Smilovichi.
Chaïm the pariah, blood and dander

drawn distractedly across his twitching
face. His blood describes a dizzy trek
between the wagon ruts where Nietzsche's

underdog progresses in the wreck
of finished business, punctuating shtetl
street with fallen drops. His chicken neck

and urchin's chest exposed above the wattle
of a tunic ripped within the hour, the boy
is beaten once again. Not by his brutal

brothers this time, but by others. Oy!
Beware obsession! For in this world are things
as likely to empower as to destroy,

a light and darkness through the land that sings
precariously in the resonance
of every day. A pendulum that swings

inside a hidden engine. There's a sense
of latent danger, violence in a law
beyond tradition, an experience

in nature and the Lord's imprimatur,
"Behold the Child".
                          Having never seen
a work of art beyond the constant noir

vignette of ghetto poverty, Soutine
compulsively confronts the world, his scrimmage
with the word of God, by drawing. Green

and gray convert to charcoal in his homage,
meanwhile flouting a severe taboo,
the second one, against the graven image.

And now, it's learned, he's sketched a learned Jew.
"As if such portraits weren't forbidden, dunce!"
The rabbi's son, the village butcher, screw-

locked, punches Chaïm and kicks him once.
The butcher's brothers throw him at the wall.
"*Frumkeit! Frumkeit, fool!*" The eldest grunts

and swings a broken pinewood board with all
the force of his observance on the slumping
boy. And then the boots. And then the crawl

toward the doorway of the shed. Then something
drops on Chaïm's back—a burlap sack
of poultry offal. Now the older boys are bumping

into one another heading back
to town, ecstatic in the rage they've spent
and laughing, satisfied with their attack.

III

At the end of the road he sees his father
sitting in a window sewing rags
and davening. Factotum to a tailor,

poor as gravel, Soutine père reneges
on any promise of Chagall nostalgia
that the shtetl might suggest. He sags

over a pile of scraps in a neuralgia
of repetitive despair. His cuff
must be avoided! Surely all the

Soutine children understand the stuff
of dreamless sleep. The ghetto's endless drone.
The heavy thud of father's mad rebuff.

But how long has Chaïm been standing there alone,
the raining shots of multicolored light
behind his eyes? He plucks a chicken bone

and feathers from his clothes as night
chokes over Smilovichi. Then she's there,
as always, to collect him. "What a sight,"

his mother says, and pushes back his hair.
And what a sight indeed. An eye is swollen
shut. He's bleeding almost everywhere,

his face, his hands. His hat is likely stolen,
"for he had one, yes, this morning, if you please!"
He isn't crying this time, though. A woolen

shawl is wrapped around him. Mother tries
to lift the boy, but at 13, her youngest son
won't budge. "He usually cries,"

she mutters to the doctor's wife who's come
to see what all the trouble is about.
"It's bad," she tells the mother—the child is dumb

and listless. "Some cuts are very deep. I doubt
they'll stop without some stitches. Let me help."
They carry him. Now half the shtetl's out

to see the doctor take the sorry whelp
indoors. A mass of beards and pipes and hats.
The donkeys haw. The scrawny street dogs yelp.

IV

For sixteen days, Soutine remains in bed
recuperating at the doctor's home—
a bed he doesn't have to share. His head

is wrapped in cotton gauze, a comb
of rooster shock protruding from the crown.
At first he worries he'll go blind and roam

the streets of Smilovichi like a clown,
a village idiot. The term had been applied
at various localities in town—

When the *schul* dismissed him, Chaïm stayed inside
and helped his father. He would watch the light,
remembering as a toddler how he'd hide

behind a chest of drawers, stay out of sight
for hours, while the window's square design
traversed the room. And now, in bed at night,

he only has to close his eyes. The fine
bouquet of pin-scratch lights still shoot and twist
inside his mind. By day, he struggles with the line,

a charcoal sprig inside his healing fist.
The springtime air outside makes slight incursions.
His mother visits once. She brings a list

and shows it to the Smilovichi surgeon.
"Your mother's going to the village council
with her case"—the doctor's wife, her words in

gentle pace, describes to him a town still
buzzing with the news of how they nearly
killed him. He considers how the town will

someday do the job and sees it clearly.
Should he heal, he'll somehow have to leave.
This incident will cost the rabbi dearly.

"The idiot gets paid! Can you believe?
As if the world were rattling with such rubles.
Soutine the mender cannot sew a sleeve—

he gets a quarter-hundred for his troubles?
Our rabbi is a fool to play along."
The muddy street of Smilovichi bubbles

for an hour. And it isn't very long
before the artist leaves the family hovel
for the school of Vilna. That's where things go wrong.

Chapter 2

The Eye that Looks

I

He sets out, first, to Minsk with Kikoïne,
the Belarusian kid intent on drawing
who one day would accompany Soutine

to France. But first to Minsk, where one heart-clawing
circumstance is traded for another.
Don't skip ahead to Montparnasse, ignoring

how the fledgling artist leaves his mother,
bounding through the ghetto's gray and green,
escaping with his underprivileged brother-

in-the-arts.
             Dear reader, have you ever seen
a baby sparrow, fallen from its nest,
attempt a running takeoff from between

the leaves and rocks? The stilted anapest
of pointy feet that somehow grab a stick
and hold the bird at momentary rest

before an uncoordinated lick
of wingwork reignites? Then you would know
how Chaïm and Kikoïne performed the trick

of forward motion from a slum. Below
the crooked roadside undergrowth they dart
from shadow into light. They stop and go.

They disappear and reemerge. They start
and startle like two mice that burrow down,
pop up and flap a wing. It is an art

the two will master: getting out of town.
"Soutine, you would have made a brilliant crook.
The prince of thieves—I'll draw for you a crown."

"For jumping into every darkened nook?
But why this in-and-out, Michel? It's crazy."
"It is better that your neighbors shouldn't look."

"But isn't that a little bit fugazy?
We do these tradesmen and their starving mules
a favor. Why?" "You know about the lazy

eye, the eye that *looks*, Soutine. The fools
that Solomon identifies, with round
and lustful eyes for idols. Beware the ghouls!"

"Apocryphal!" "So what? It gets around!
And what about the pregnant girl. One look
at some old milk cow and she found

a bullock in her bassinet. She took
a chance and got a monster for her pains."
"Another bit of bullshit for the book.

Look, Kikoïne, you are a man with brains.
And Smilovichi is a memory.
We'll walk to Minsk, and then we'll take the trains.

We'll be in Vilna soon. Just wait and see.
And please, Michel, forget the *mishegas*.
Here comes another schlepper. Follow me!"

He hops behind a wall of stone and moss
and rolls under a haystack in the yard.
Michel is quick to follow. Now they toss

from stack to stack. They keep on guard
and out of sight. This isn't superstition.
Never. But it certainly dies hard.

II

Kikoïne adjusts his wireframe glasses,
pokes his hat back and exhales a puff
of acrid smoke. The evening passes

as he contemplates his colleague's rough
portfolio. "A portrait. This one's good,"
he smiles and holds it up. "Not good enough,"

Soutine replies. "Your mother, no? You should
take better care of these," says Kikoïne.
Our sulking hero throws a piece of wood

onto a fire that tosses sparks between
the tree line and the bonework of a shack
abandoned long ago. A common scene

along the road to Minsk. A bivouac.
"Tomorrow we shall come to Minsk from Pinsk ,"
jokes Kikoïne, putting the pictures back

into a burlap bag. *Be ready, Minsk !"*
No luck. Soutine is going dark again,
a heavy scowl across a countenance

of shadows in the dusk. "Good night, my friend."
A sparking pipe is tapped against a rock—
the Belarusian diplomat knows when

to call it quits with Chaïm, when to walk
away. He climbs into the broken shed
and curls up in his overcoat, the clock

of constellations ticking overhead.
Meanwhile Chaïm himself is dozing off,
the cooling embers hardening to lead

beside him where he lies. His bed is rough,
but certainly he's used to making do.
His dreams are made of harder stuff—

the beating of a wing, metallic blue
against the broken brickwork wall.
His brothers' surly voices breaking through

the darkness. Talons whip above it all
as, screeching horribly, a hanging fowl
explodes in gold and red. His dreams recall

his punishment. The hours inside a foul
enclosure, locked in by his brothers, turn
into nocturnal theater, a hole,

a veil of echoes where the pendant churns,
the dying poultry framed against the fallen
brick, behind which, black, eternal, burns

an empty hell. He hears his mother calling
"Chaïm!" and sees the milk and Russian bread
laid out for him below the shock of crawling

flesh and whirling feathers overhead.
He tries to move, but everything is stiff,
his arms are paralyzed, his legs are dead.

III

Kikoïne awakes and wonders if
Soutine has slept at all. He's not surprised
to find the portrait of Chaïm's mother ripped,

and burned and booted, for the cries
at dawn were not those of the crested cock.
His friend sits on the road with bloated eyes.

Chapter 3

Vilna

I

Cigarettes and alcohol alight and snap
the air like wings. But the Ažuolas Canteen
is nearly empty. Sullen drinkers nap

as pictures from the new machine
ignite the wall and other drinkers gape.
The young projectionist—is that Soutine?—

keeps fumbling with a reel of film and tape.
Repairs are handled on the fly tonight.
And yes, that *is* Soutine.
                                    The late escape

from Smilovichi swung through Minsk, all right,
where Kikoïne made good on his connection.
Herr Kruger took them in and taught, despite

his feeble grasp, the elements of sketching.
"Guaranteed Success in Just Three Months,"
his advertisement read. His chronic kvetching

was a nuisance, but he threw in lunch
and something like supplies. They paid
him five of Chaïm's rubles, which was much

more than they'd hoped to pay. But then, they stayed
with him most nights. It worked out rather well.
The prints he showed them, soiled and decayed,

were inspiration. And they worked like hell
at drawing still lifes on the kitchen table.
Basic shapes. Proportions. Charcoal fell

on paper under frenzied hands, unstable
gestures, and those red and bloated eyes.
And something came of it. They were able

to amass portfolios that would comprise
their first successful pictures. When they left
for Vilna in the fall, the czarist skies

portentous, granite gray, the fields bereft
of April's camouflage, they had the skills
prerequisite to managing the heft

of academic training. And in Vilna
they'd meet other Jewish refugees
with piles of drawings. Brotherhood instills

a sense of common purpose, and for these
unwanted brothers of the shtetl, art
meant life or death, or an incurable disease.

II

The flame. The flame of hunger and a flame
behind the cranking wheel. Electric light
and pale light in the alley are the same,

distinguished from the darkness, from the night
he followed Pinchus to the prostitutes
and found his level: *"You're gonna be all right"*—

Pinchus Krémègne (the name means *flint*) could shoot
between the shadows thrown outside the doors,
around the pimps and barmen in cahoots

with matrons at the black hotels. The whores
and clientele, as in some fevered dream,
streamed by the darkened windows of the stores

in waves of laughter. *"Follow me, Soutine."*
The alley stairs led to a lighted cell.
He followed. "Where the hell is Kikoïne?"

"Delayed," said Pinchus, who had seen Michel
engage with business in the street. The rain
had stopped, but in the lamp-lit gutter swell

a world of water tumbled like Champagne,
a glistening red and gold, into the sewer.
Soutine ascended slowly with Krémègne,

his champion, the lanky connoisseur
and quaffer of mundane Shiraz. The girls
from Latvia, a highlight on the tour,

in fact the final stop, wore dime store pearls
and welcomed them in broken French. Soutine
stood silently before their flesh and curls,

his tongue and ample lips in an obscene
arrangement as Krémègne engaged the chrysalis
beauties in the usual routine

of haggling. The preliminary business.
"Do you talk?" The short one spoke in Russian
as she sidled toward Soutine. "Hey, is this

young man an idiot?" The blunt percussion
of the working women's cackling laughter
cracked the air and landed like a punch on

something in Chaïm's gullet. "Is he daft, or ...?"
"No! My friend's from Smilovichi!!!" Pinchus
chucked him on the shoulder. Some time after

Pinchus took the tall one to a bed behind the sink,
his pants around his ankles, Chaïm engaged
the short one in some fondling. You would think

his background was in sideshow wrestling staged
to entertain a troop of clowns in training.
The woman, Myra, heavyset and aged

perhaps 18, was not one for complaining.
It seemed this boy would finish all too soon,
pay up and leave. And in the time remaining

she could smoke that cigarette the skinny one
proffered on entering. But Chaïm's moves
relaxed into caresses, slow, immune

to the reality, the smell of love's
detritus in the broken, unmade bed,
the sores that looked like acid burns, the grooves

and bluing in the woman's flesh. Instead,
the sensory composite registered
as "mother," "nurse." The nightmare of the shed

resolved to woman's consolation. And he heard
her saying something in a foreign tongue.
His face was nestled in her breasts. The word

she said was *copilul*, a word among
some others in Romanian—her pedigree
was mixed. Obliterated. She was young

and lost and close to death. And so was he.
The woman rubbed his shoulder and he came.
She crushed her cigarette—to some degree

she came as well. The flame is still a flame
and Myra, still a girl, was not quite nearly
dead as her colleague underneath Krémègne

(who also seemed to speak in tongues). Severely
shaken up, Soutine, embarrassed by
his raptured accident, saw things more clearly.

Details surfaced in the artist's eye
as images and feelings snapped and burned.
He covered up his face as if to cry.

But Myra was intolerant. "You'll learn,"
she said to him in words he understood,
"to get more for your rubles in return."

III

The puppet dog rides downtown in a truck.
He jumps into the street and nips a heel.
He has to save the little girl! Good luck,

O mascot, teeth sunk in an orange peel
and bounding through the world of animated
bones—a pheasant and a fish—and real

Beelzebub and Belial.
                As stated,
Chaïm has found employment in the city.
He is moderately compensated

for projecting fantasies. A shitty
job, the hours of cranking celluloid
across the incandescent fire. Did he

appreciate the stories as he toyed
with the mechanics from behind the desk?
Tonight, the Ažuolas Canteen enjoys

the films of Wladyslaw Starewicz,
The Cameraman's Revenge and now *The Mascot*.
A flashing light on our projectionist

portends a futuristic camera shot
by Leni Riefenstahl. The up-lit grimace.
But it moves in disjunct pictures, not

the smooth stop-action of the carapace
and dragonfly canoodling in the hotel room.
A violent portrait sequence fills a space

of abstract forms restrictive as a tomb
and open as a thunderstorm. Our hero
is inscrutable and rapt and, we assume,

transported by the fantasy, the zero
gravity and killing weight of nature,
as he fiddles with the new machine like Nero.

Or ... is there another kind of rapture
anchored to the outcome of a dream,
to an image no machine will ever capture?

Chapter 4

*U*topia

I

Krémègne presents with an archaic nude
in plaster. Kikoïne a village square,
Soutine, an unconventional *étude*

d'atelier—a table setting with a pear,
a cup, a bottle, and a carving knife.
Supremely gestural, despite the spare

arrangement. Little "stillness" in this "life."
Pinchus and Michel share sidelong glances
understanding that their friend is off

the mark for the assignment. That his chances
for matriculating are ... extreme.
"But, Pinchus, look at how his picture dances."

"Yes, I know. He's had it, Kikoïne."
"I give him credit, nonetheless." "Here goes."
The drawing master enters: *"Chaïm Soutine!"*

Krémègne and Kikoïne assume the pose
and brace for the ordeal of academe.
"Do yourself a favor, wipe your nose,"

a whispering Pinchus turns the mise-en-scène
as Chaïm advances to the doctor's chair,
the final act in a recurrent dream.

"Monsieur Soutine, agent provocateur,
has played the *Fauve*," Professor Klosser tells
the class. "But we do not so easily scare!"

*   *   *

II

On Saturdays, the L.A. cabs get lost,
requiring passengers to navigate.
The City of Angels has a holocaust

museum ... but where the fuck? It's getting late,
and I fly early from this landscape reminiscent
of a Jersey parking lot. But wait.

According to the map, my driver isn't
thudding reggae to some outer shire
of strip malls in the Santa Clara desert.

"Isn't that the LACMA?" I inquire—
an art museum that might have decent art.
"Matisse and Company," the weekend flyer

from the Marriott proclaimed. *"The Heart
of Modernism Beats Downtown!"* Well, it has to
beat performing in this D'Oyly Carte

production of *Utopia.* "Just past the
Burger King, you make a right," says I,
de facto navigator on the raft of

the *Medusa.* Beneath a reddened autumn sky
infused with city light, he lets me off
and soon I'm mixing with the hoi polloi

outside the old museum. Time enough
to catch the sunset with the cognoscenti
on the plaza underneath "The Fauve

Landscape."

        This was the fall of 1990,
and I felt the charge of a decade's change
well up as Angelo Badalamenti

played through the PA. I loved his strange
progressions, so familiar now, but then ...
a sense of hope and mystery, a range

of open possibilities, a pen,
a sheet of paper, and a waiting world
were laid before me in L.A. Again,

I read the banner. *Fauve.* Its colors hurled
against the purple field of falling night
and shadowed trees. Truth is, I'd never heard

the word before. But soon I'd see the light
of "wild beasts." Matisse, Vlaminck, Derain,
Marquet, Dufy, van Dongen, Braque, Valtat ...

III

My first encounter, very much a birth,
involved an acclimation to the light
and color in a room. The planet earth

reformed with everything unnamed and right
before my eyes. Van Gogh, of course,
the obvious association—night

of stars, a field of flowers, louvered doors
upon a harbor as the details rose
in yellows, reds, and blues. A thermador

20

of hues, a luscious world uncalculated
in the gesture of a loaded brush,
the seven galleries were populated

with pictorial creation. Blush
and blackness, complementary red and green—
its language came upon me in a rush.

Nature as I felt it must be seen
expressed in kind, as the ineffable
but known. Behind the age of the machine,

beyond the chemistry, a decibel
above and one below. The everything—
the air, the earth, the wind, and bloody hell.

*   *   *

IV

"Good morning, Chaïm. Drunk again last night?"
Krémègne inspects the unhygienic fellow
curled against the wall. "A little tight,

perhaps? … Soutine? … " He pulls aside the yellow
bedding to reveal his friend, unconscious,
face down on a dark blue stain. "… Hello!",

Krémègne intones, confronted with a noxious
odor and a momentary shot
of terror alternating at the nexus

of inevitable night, a knot
untied, a rope that slips into the void.
Adrenalin takes over. Blood and snot

and vomit; Chaïm's oddly mongoloid
expression—certainly the kid is dead.
Krémègne's first aid, intuitive, deployed

amid the tangled sweeps of black and red,
elicits a response at last. A gasp
and a convulsive start. The soiled bed

disgorges Chaïm, who mumbles, in a rasp
and gurgle, something about writing home.
Michel and Pinchus lift their friend and clasp

their hands to carry him. The sodden gnome
is deadweight on the stairs. At least he's breathing
regularly—bubbles break in foam

across his swollen lips and nose. The seething
mass of pain still gnawing in his gut,
Soutine is coming to. "I think I'm bleeding."

"Yes, you are," says Kikoïne. "A lot."
"We're taking you across the street," Krémègne,
in charge, declares. "I think Dimitri's got

a doctor friend." And now the stomach pain
is sharpening. Soutine is coughing blood.
The morning street is glistening in the rain

and Vilna shudders in the fog and mud,
expressive steeples, public squares emerging
in the sullied light before the flood.

V

A room, not squalid but unkempt. A place
to work. A window open in the hall.
Our hero registers a new disgrace:

22

An ulcer, meaning no more alcohol.
The doctor made it clear. And certain food
is henceforth off the table. Smokes as well,

he told him. "Now you've something real to brood
about,"—Krémègne, attempting levity.

In bleak November, this is where things stood:

The drawings Chaïm brought to the committee
for admissions at the college split
the vote. Professor Klosser, in his snitty

manner, recommended "non-admit."
However, Dr. Klein said not so fast.
"Based on what he's shown us, I'll commit

to stamping his enrollment once he's passed
a regimen of basic drawing. Klosser?"
"Doctor, I believe my vote is cast."

Not inclined to overrule the tosser,
Klein suggests that the panel interviews
the applicant. "He either comes across or

else he's out. Feel free to run him through
the mill on his philosophy, technique.
Quite honestly, I'm sensing there's a true

ability behind his, shall we say, unique
approach to drawing." Klein holds rather firm,
and Chaïm is called before the board that week.

And by the end of May, he'll close the term
with much to show. Some thirty canvases
that writhe in Klosser's studio. A germ

of genius sprouting from this little man with his
propensity for pleading. And his knack
for tantrums. "Almost self-destructive, this

Soutine," thinks Klosser. "Witness his attack
in oil on panel!" Lifting a tableau
of winding stairs along a railroad track,

"We'll see what comes of this." He'll never know
what comes, of course. Soutine works hard at Vilna.
He is well aware of where he needs to go.

*   *   *

VI

Near Paris, a commuter train breaks down
and sets the stage for an encounter fraught
with comic elegance: A factory town

five miles from the city; two painters caught
up in the hike of angry men in suits—
André Derain, Maurice de Vlaminck. A hot

September afternoon. Of all the shared pursuits
identifiable beneath the sun,
painting might put strangers in cahoots

most readily. "Monsieur, is that a gun?"
the jovial Vlaminck, to break the ice,
enquires of Derain's rig. "It looks like one."

"My fellow traveler," Derain replies,
"At last, a chance to introduce ourselves.
I see you're also fully armed." The skies,

24

a mix of evening clouds on ochre shelves
of factory exhaust, the darkling rows
of cypress trees inclining, summer swells.

The color waits in hiding. Heaven knows
how daily circumstances set the pace
and draw the lines of history. The story goes,

these painters set a date to paint. A place
selected for its elemental charm—
some workmen on a towpath (yes, a trace

of the pedestrian), a lake, a farm
and the eternal drama. Inner light
and color. It would sound like an alarm

inaudible, innate, untied across the white
support that glimmers through the steady rain
of pure vermilion, green and gold.

                                    "All right,"
I'm thinking, gaslight shining from the Seine
across my L.A. cab, the factoid plaques
in play, "It starts on a commuter train."

BOOK

II

Chapter 1

The Room Upstairs

I

The suits were throwing rock at ABC
and the economy was running stupid
with the scissors. They'd done the deal with Disney

and the glossy magazine I edited
was moved to Philadelphia. *So long!*,
I said. But the Philly honchos thought it

might make sense to keep a Falun Gong
of editors online in NYC.
The boys in Philadelphia were wrong,

in my assessment. They encouraged me
to take up golf! O Philadelphia,
behind your moat of mediocrity,

your Main Line harboring a mafia
of thug execs with big chips on the shoulders
of their plastic suits! "Just keep on top of your

constituency, serve the stakeholder
and stay in touch with Al in advertising."
"... Got it, George." The autumn nights grew colder

as they do. I wintered, realizing
that the center had been pulled apart.
A visit from the junta, not surprising

when it came in March, would mark the start
of double sessions in the studio,
my garret library and world of art.

Not long before the bastards let me go,
I'd followed through on my epiphany
in California, and the status quo

got complicated. Putting up with me
and all my sacks of pricey oil paint,
my disappearing acts, would prove to be

impossible. And Maureen to be a saint—
she stuck around, despite my tendency
to disengage. This was not without complaint,

of course, nor I above mendacity
explaining where I'd go. In fact, I'd changed.
Not realizing my capacity

for utter selfishness I'd rearranged
my whole routine. The world revolved around
my studies on New Jersey Transit trains,

museum hooky, and the ups and downs
of learning how to paint at 33,
alone. So when the Pennsylvania clowns

explained that they were getting rid of me,
my heart rejoiced. My mind took care of all
the worrying. My afternoons were free

as were my mornings. And I talked to Paul,
a painter friend who told me, "Keep it simple.
Reds and blues and yellows. You can call

me any time." His work set an example—
I had seen it years before I met the Fauves.
I thought about it as I combed that temple

of my late conversion in L.A., which proves
its quality. I scumbled through a string
of summer days and nights. The basic truths

in nature I'd ignored, aroused, were rendering
my mind a shambles and my heart a slave.
I felt the force of a vocation bending

every narrow road I'd tried to pave
according to a teleology
beyond my grasp. The whole Platonic cave,

the pure objective subjectivity,
as Paul described it. All-engaging work.
I caught my breath again, eventually,

but not before I had my little perk—
the unemployed guy with an easel,
going Fauvist at the station. Clerk

and passenger appalled, I painted diesel
engines—railroad niceties be damned!
Derided by commuting students, evil

bastards, I persisted. And, as planned,
I finally set my easel at the Met
to copy the Pissarro barges. Panned

or praised (opinions varied), I would get
the juices flowing, palette fat with oils,
standing on a canvas drop cloth wet

and Pollock-like with drips and coils
of swirling excess, yellow, blue, and red.
Astonishing. "You got a lot of balls,"

a voice amid the choir behind me said.
But I was with Pissarro at the time.
Of course, my upstairs room was overhead—

I had to find a job or turn to crime.
Deciding for the former, I returned,
pro forma, to the old commuter grind.

*   *   *

II

"*La gloria di colui che tutto move*
  per l'universo penetra, e risplende
  in una parte piú e meno altrove
Ne ceil che piú de la sua luce prende
  fu' io, e vide cose che redire
  né sa né può chi di là sù discende ... "

Dante's *Paradise*, or *Up from Fire*.
Modigliani would recite it when
the line between the object and desire

was all too recognizable. And then
he'd laugh. Not every model satisfied
his ideal notion. Maybe one in ten.

Not every naked woman that he eyed
through midnight sessions mattered more
than practice on the human form, applied

theatrics, textbook odalisques in poor
portrayals. The sitting didn't always end
in *Priapus Unbound*, the paramour

32

resplendent on the red divan, pretend
bohemia behind the artist's curtain.
Of course it didn't. Nor do I intend

to bust the myth, as any myth is certain
to have spun from an essential truth.
He could recite at length in perfect Latin.

Tall, Italian, a Sephardic Jew,
the aura of Romanticism hovers
on such tousled manes. And, yes, a few

of the divine reclining nudes were lovers.
And some put in the extra hour where
they sprawled for him. Some turned him down, and others

got the Dante treatment. Here and there
a legend falls to flesh on a recliner.
A modeled breast, a bended knee, the hair

line on the ochre lips of the vagina.
The subtle smile and raptured eyes that soften,
tending to dissolve in cobalt china

pools of satisfaction. You can often
get a sense of whether the impasto
paradise was painted just before the toss in

crimson comforters and sheets, or after.
And all too often, if you listen closely,
you can hear the Dante and the laughter.

III

13 Rue Ravigan, *la Butte Montmartre*,
a low-slung building that the poet Max
ordained "the laundry boat:" Bateau-Lavoir.

Cezanne, the caustic hermit, died in Aix
the year Modigliani sang his song in
terza rima as he joined the Pax

Diaspora—Picasso, Gris, van Dongen—
in an ark that launched a century of blood
and anarchy. *"Nel mezzo del cammin ..."*

He heard an echo in the stones and wood.
He found the amber light of stony Italy
in hilly streets. His boots were caked with mud,

his dreams, before the drugs, with poetry.
With Dante and d'Annunzio. He'd scan
a constant line of classic prosody

and carry it subconsciously to canvas,
to the nude on his divan. Vlaminck,
years later, holding court at Au Lapin

Agile: "Modigliani laid a franc
upon the table, and he'd sketch the ladies.
They would pay. And he might thank

them later in his atelier. As I have said, his
corner of the laundry boat produced
a lot of dirty laundry." "Overrated,"

came a curt reply—Vlaminck reduced
that amateur to sulking tweeds with just
a stare. "My friend, the women he seduced

are classic treasures, held for us in trust."
A nascent avant-garde, beguiled by cubes,
was tearing down the Louvre and making dust

of the Uffizi, skewering the "rubes
of the academy." But the dark Italian
had his own café, where cones and tubes

and cubic forms that march like a battalion
of refracting mirrors—circus balls,
and broken glass from a disjointed galleon

on Rue Ravigan—engaged him not at all.
And when Umberto Boccioni paid
his fellow-countryman-abroad a call,

Modigliani shook his hand and said
he wasn't used to joining clubs
or signing manifestos. Black and red

and white. An amber atmosphere that rubs
its color into vibrant browns and grays
around the edges of the potted shrubs

and windowed bakeries defined his days
in pictures that amalgamated all
of Paris. All the ghostly émigrés

that walked the streets or lined the plaster walls
of the enchanted arrondissement kept
him up at night. By now the alcohol

was taking hold of him. And if he slept,
it would be slumped below a canvas wet
with color in a simple room he swept

and cleaned—he didn't have a roommate yet.
The space was his alone. He hung up prints,
the masters, wall to wall, his palette set

in earth tones mixed from yellows, reds, and glints
of cobalt china blue. He painted faces,
people, nudes. And he'd spend time with friends,

Max Jacob and Picasso, who knew places
in the city that sold wooden masks
from Africa. They'd peruse the cases

of antique and tribal helmets and the casks
and coffins at the Louvre. They'd get drunk
and prowl the boulevard in haughty masques,

enacting an impromptu play. They stank
of Le Bateau-Lavoir. And everything
converged on canvas or a chiseled hunk

of stone. Modigliani would begin to sing
again, he'd leave the crowd and concentrate
on the Italian ritual to which he'd bring

a mask or model in a heightened state
of consciousness achieved in reverie.
He'd work. And at the end he'd contemplate

a night's creation and the panoply
of masterworks converging on his wall.
The One. The sacrament of constancy.

*   *   *

IV

At 1 a.m., the smell of fish and oils
amalgamate, convincing me I've truly
nailed my subject. But the fish recoils

36

(the real one on the table). I am cruelly
made aware, as I distinguish odors,
that the painted fish is stiff. My drooling

model mocks me, as if giving orders:
Sacrifice my ass for art, OK.
But look at me from time to time! My quarters

reconcile with earthly disarray.
I'm disabused, exhausted, late for
work before I know it, and the day

swims under water. In an altered state or
out to lunch, I maunder to the Modern,
where I climb on board the escalator.

       Long before they put away the god in
the machine, before the recent renovation,
MoMA was a seminar—you'll pardon

how I put this—of religious education
in the pan-religious, humanistic sense.
It has now become a mawkish imitation

of its former self. But I'll relent.
The MoMA in the early 1990s
introduced me to a parliament

of errant knights on garrulous Rocinantes.
Van Dongen, Munch, Picasso and Matisse.
Modigliani. The Petrarchs and the Dantes

of ineffable expressions in the trees
and on the waters, spread across the table.
Braques, Bonnards, Kokoschkas and Kandinskys.

I stood for hours devouring the sable
spread beneath Modigliani's gorgeous nude,
the apricot impasto flesh, unable

to unwind. The odalisque and oud
beside her (the Matisse) would bring me down
or hold me at a steady altitude.

I'd find another gallery—the Rouault clown,
his punished Christ, his dancer with the dog.
A rotting world of jewels against the brown

and gray I'd one day see in Paris. I'd log
the names of artists. I'd accumulate
associations, and I'd later slog

through subway stations with an altered gait,
my mind on monographs I carried home.
Those days it was impossible to sate

my appetite for modern art. I'd comb
the galleries beyond my given hour
engaged with color in the cracking loam

on canvases and boards. I would admire
one landscape near the end of every visit.
The artist's name seemed somehow unfamiliar

every time I read the plaque. It didn't
stick. The chalky mill in extremis
distracted me. The lava under wizened

evergreens and the bizarre catalysis
of crazing sky and undulating hills ...
describing it, it seems ridiculous.

But every time I saw it I felt chills.
I couldn't look away. I let it churn
and work its color and its folding rills

into my consciousness. I let it burn.
Again, I'd read the ghostly name: *Soutine*.
Modigliani's roommate, I would learn.

*   *   *

Chapter 2

The Hive

I

"Hold still a minute now. And stop your screaming."
Foujita's tweezers poke the fleshy molding
of a dirty ear. Modigliani's seeming

nonchalance belies his effort, holding
the tormented Belarus against
a mattress in this battle scene unfolding—

Chaïm screams, *"I'll go insane!"* His friends,
exhausted, watch the Japanese maneuver
cautiously until the shrieking ends

with the extraction of a roach. "Whoever
says Soutine keeps to himself should try
to sleep next door," Krémègne, a bit hung over,

groans on leaving. The fear in Chaïm's eye
subsides in increments as Modigliani
breaks his wrestler's hold and lets him lie

across the elevated pallet, an uncanny
rig the two assemble every night
between the rusted vats of paraffin they

situate to block the bugs that bite
(and now we must say *burrow*) as Chaïm is sleeping.
Foujita watches quietly, despite

the shock of having just removed a creeping
insect from this fellow's ear: "Soutine,
I wonder if this monster is worth keeping."

40

He drops it in an empty turpentine
container. "It looks a little like a lobster,
huh? *Still Life in a Tin Tureen.*"

Chaïm does his best through broken sobs to
thank Foujita. Modigliani calms
his friend. "Foujita, you have stopped a

genius falling from the edge. Embalm
the bug we shall, Monsieur!" "You owe me, Modi."
"Yes! Goodnight, Foujitasan!" "Shalom."

II

So. The cleanest man in Paris and the foulest
share a coffin in that famous hive,
La Ruche, in Montparnasse. The rounded palace

from the Paris Expo was a dive
for starving artists, including a cabal
of Russian émigrés. The famous five:

Jacques Lipchitz, Michel Kikoïne, Chagall,
Krémègne and Chaïm Soutine. Behind the door
of every shotgun studio, on every wall,

hung masterworks, their masters rather poor—
Brancusi, Pechstein, Delaunay, Léger,
Apollinaire, Rivera.... There were more.

La Ruche, a wine rotunda at the fair,
was built by Gustave Eiffel, disassembled
by the sculptor/fireman Boucher,

and moved across the Seine to make a temple,
a roundhouse seminary for the artists
pouring into Paris. They'd assemble

at Gare Montparnasse, debarking to the hardest
life imaginable, not unlike ascetic
clergy, driven as the Bonapartists,

dedicated to a grand aesthetic.
Having done the three-year course at Vilna,
Chaïm joined his friends and, through poetic

chance, Modigliani at La Ruche.
They say that opposites attract each other,
and they do. But a magnetic push

and pull much stronger often brings a brother
to an unmet brother. Genius, maybe.
Dreams, obsessions, or a knack for spitting blood.

Modigliani's movements are a mystery
and Chaïm's as well. And so they come together
in the storied oblong box of misery

and bliss. At night, Modigliani reads the
classics to his protégé. Or Nietzsche:
"That which doesn't kill us makes us stronger."

III

Another portrait. Charcoal-shadowed eyes,
unruly hair, despite the perfect part—
a poet dressed in anarchist disguise?

But the hands give him away. An artist's heart
is manifest in slender hands like these:
a portrait of the painter dying for his art

at the café. Some worker buys him cheese
and coffee—he's been slouching there all day
against the counter, not so much as "please,"

but clearly bumming for café au lait,
a sandwich from some sympathetic soul.
"All right. But does he have to dress that way?"

"They say he's an eccentric. He's a Pole
or Russian. Anyway, a Jew." Soutine
today has taken long johns, cut a hole

around the crotch, and made a shirt. "I've seen
him here before. He's absolutely filthy."

France had gone to war. Such wraiths were seen

and tolerated in cafés. Unhealthy
waifs and workers. Chaïm qualified
as both. A railroad porter serving wealthy

passengers, he'd earned enough to tide
him over after paying his tuition
at the workshop of Cormon. The tide

had turned at *that* Parisian institution,
where van Gogh had only made a dent.
The Modern line was coming to fruition,

and the luminary partisans who went
to study with the master brought a new
perspective and a new aesthetic bent

toward individual expression. Few
among the acolytes in Paris at that time
were unaffected by Cezanne. The true

religion had been loosed. But Chaïm
knew enough to take advantage of
his access to tradition. The sublime

experience of visiting the Louvre
enthralled him to the masters. Jean Fouquet,
Chardin, Courbet. And his obsessive love

could drive him to distraction. He would stay
for hours in one gallery and daven
as he strained to take things in in such a way

that he'd see everything. A kind of heaven
clouded overhead but out of reach.
He combed the earthly shadows of the seven

rays through every hall. Beyond all speech,
he struggled to communicate with saints
and get a take on God they didn't teach

in Smilovichi. The ray fish worked in paints
that glistened jewel-like symbolized the Christ—
a still life by Chardin. Immense constraints

evaporated in the colors sliced
and spread on shanks of raw and bleeding meat.
Take Rembrandt's hanging carcass, which enticed

him more than anything. He couldn't eat,
but he could try to paint the butchered world.
He stumbled every evening through the street,

compelled and anguished, hungry, and he hurled
himself at canvases at night. The war
progressed. He worked at digging trenches, curled

into his own anxiety the more
he labored and the less he ate, as if
some wolf were waiting just outside the door.

IV

"As if," however, pales before the "is."
His art does not describe hallucination.
Despite the harrowed forms, remember this:

He painted nothing from imagination.
The rictus maw and guttered eyes of cod
derive from hours of work and contemplation

of a fish, his situation, and the God
he couldn't reach. He laid things on the table
or saw them in the market, like the scrod,

Chianti bottles, bread in veritable
landscapes. Turnips cracked, extraordinary
carrots bolting out like orange cable

through the mounds of brown and green. The very
thought of food would make him dizzy. He
was starving in a bourgeois bestiary,

an unstable feast, deprived by poverty
and something tearing, always, at his gut.
He didn't have a franc. He couldn't eat,

and he was not supposed to drink. He'd glut
himself on visions in his deprivation
and a ratty overcoat. He suffered, but

he painted. Nothing from imagination—
he painted from experience, direct
involvement, aching need, and a fixation.

Chapter 3

Monster

I

Baudelaire advised us to be drunk
at every hour of the day on wine
or virtue. Or on poetry. He sank

into his rapture. But here we have Soutine,
who's drinking mostly milk when he can get it,
staggering about the public green,

a color somewhat reticent. The setting
sun is only hinted at behind
the weathered Luxembourg. A fetid

overcoat and winter fog, combined,
equate him with the landscape. There's obsession.
That's intoxication. Never mind

his lapses with the bottle. No depression,
but a steady, tense anxiety. The bell
at Église Saint-Sulpice will close this session

near the still and childless carousel.
Later with Modigliani at La Ruche
there is the semiweekly show-and-tell.

"You take the cake as always, *sac de puce*."
"The cake? I wish," Soutine, a sheepish grin,
well, maybe goatish, mumbles.
"Call a truce!"—

Krémègne arrives. "But Pinchus, look at him!
He hasn't had a drink. Now ... look at *this!*"
Modigliani motions to a scrim

Soutine has pinned against a rotting piece
of broken pasteboard over which he's painted
herrings in a thickly oiled frieze,

a meal wrapped in a nightmare—no doubt tainted
fish. "I see such things when I've been smoking,
usually at the point of fainting.

And his landscapes—more like when I'm drinking.
But Soutine? I watch him work. He's sober.
Sober, but there's something else ... " "No joking,"

says Krémègne, who looks the painting over.
"I've watched him paint a fish or two myself."
The studio, perennial October,

generates a mauve and auburn warmth
in February. Amedeo's nudes,
his working palettes stacked upon a shelf,

contribute to the ambiance. Études
and caryatids. Works in progress. Women.
Venal sex. A luxury exudes,

amid the smell of oil, from canvas hung on
poorly plastered walls. Modigliani
vets a village scene by Kikoïne,

Krémègne's still life—a large one of a coffee
pot with flowers, a teacup and a kettle—
and Soutine's portrait of a nurse. This man he

shares his floor with and the other shtetl
Jews share something quite ineffable.
A common touch on subjects that unsettle

even as they coax a voluble
reaction one would only call surrender—
a heavy sigh of inexplicable

despair and resignation. Chaïm's slender
hand curls nervously into his hair
as he regards Modigliani's tender

gaze. But it's an enigmatic stare
that Modi fixes on the wide-eyed nurse.
Her Russian countenance. A sad affair.

II

The face of Anna Akhmatova glides
above the boulevards in early June.
Through Paris, 1910. Nikolai Gumilev guides

her past Les Deux Magots to a commune
of Russian intellectuals abroad.
A tall and graceful beauty, she's immune

to the attention that the boulevard
bestows. Indeed, Parisian heads are turning.
A beguilement of scarves, a corded

coat and tunic—Anna has discerning
taste. Her husband navigates the crowd
of preening dilettantes. Tonight he's learning

how the French can get particularly loud
in their regard for women. He's a poet.
He would seem above it all, that cloud

of jealousy about his eyes, that note
of worry not withstanding. He endures
her opulence. He grieves, but doesn't show it

through the days and weeks, the steady course
of revolutionary fervor and debate,
of poetry and art behind the doors

of the salon. Then, one night, very late
he spies his wife conversing with that young
Italian who's been coming 'round. Sedate,

well-bred, a Jewish artist, he is one
of the Montmartre antagonists. He seems
an intellectual. He's no Don Juan.

And Gumilev looks on as Anna beams
and nods. She lays her hand on the Italian's.
That's innocent enough. So pleasant dreams,

poor Nikolai Gumilev....
                         The salon's
gaslight flares to morning rays on Anna
and Modigliani by the sculpted stallions

in the Tuileries. Tolstoy's Karenina
has nothing on the poet's wife, who'll one day
rise as Russia's finest poet. On a

public bench, they share their time and sundry
observations upon poetry and art
against the bright vignette of sails and Sunday

painters circling the fountain. In her heart,
the poet opens to the painter's spirit.
A beguilement of scarves is pulled apart.

III

If Anna's taken by the spirit of the age,
her lover will be taken even faster.
Her husband, Nikolai, will leave the stage

by night. But, first, their marriage. A disaster.
From Paris to St. Petersburg, and soon
a diplomatic junket's on his roster.

"His passion fades," she writes. "The honeymoon
is over." Fair enough. At any rate,
she leaves for Paris at the end of June.

Connections at the Russian consulate
arrange for an apartment, and she joins
Modigliani, who could hardly wait.

In his recent letters, Modi coins
a phrase. *Vous êtes en moi comme une
hantise.* "You are my obsession." Well, once

a *peintre maudit,* one is likely to remain one.
Cursed. The painter as a portrait of Rimbaud.
Again they sit together in the sun,

but now they have another place to go
where Anna poses, first for pencil sketches.
Later, there are sessions in his studio.

Anna Akhmatova, one imagines, stretches
out across the red divan at Le Bateau-
Lavoir. A golden August sunset catches

her reclining form, enough to show
the surface contrasts in varieties
of ochre red and gold. The subtle glow

and ballast of her breasts. The subtleties
that elevate the nude to the supreme
accomplishment in Western art. A tease,

but nothing vulgar. Anna is sublime—
She leaves the scene to our imagination,
as does Amedeo. Not a line

of any kind in curatorial description—
coffee table book, museum plaque—
identifies a nude in this position

as Anna Akhmatova. But the lack
of positive ID means next to nothing.
All the nudes are titled *Nude*, in fact.

Admirers will find that vague, subjective "something,"
an amber highlight at the mouth, the pallor
of the thighs against the scarlet bunting.

And there is that portrait with the outré collar,
Anna Akhmatova, fully dressed,
a formal sitting in a bourgeois parlor.

But enough of speculation. It is best
at some point to refer to documents.
And much of Anna's writing does attest

to an affair. She speaks of daily sacraments,
of ritual encounters. She's discreet ....
I'll paraphrase a diary entry meant

to settle scores. "I heard him in the sleeping street,
a specter's footfall. One could sense his shadow.
His silhouette against the blinds. We'd meet

in a café at midnight in a sad old
corner of *le 4e arrondissement.*
A solitary 'victim of Picasso,'

he reviled all fashion. Modi sought
unworldly beauty in a world of the mundane.
He spoke of poetry. Sometimes he'd draw

the stragglers while reciting Paul Verlaine.
He was noble, courteous. He worked in stone,
an Italian master. Modigliani wasn't vain.

One Saturday, he went to the Salon
des Independants. He asked me to come along, and
I agreed to meet him. He was not alone.

He'd come with Jean Cocteau and Kees van Dongen.
Later on, he walked me to the Louvre.
To the Egyptian wing. He dreamed in ruins,

projecting forward, following his love
of the antique onto the streets below.
I'd know these streets, the *clair de lune* above

the Seine, the labor of the studio.
He said that women worthy of his brush
seem heavy in their clothes. Such braggadocio

becomes appropriate to one whose touch,
refined and delicate, attuned to beauty,
could alarm and soothe the stars. A Ballets Russes

of belladonna angles lay in ruddy
blankets on his easels and his wall.
One night I wandered restless through a muddy

street and through the darkness of it all
to find his hovel locked. I threw roses
idly through a window. 'How the hell

did you get in?' he later asked me. I suppose his
shock at seeing flowers rankled. My answer:
I did *not* get in. 'But every rose is

laying perfectly arranged, a floral Montserrat,
a landscape on my bed.' He took me there,
my prince, the so-called alcoholic monster."

IV

Beatrice Hastings sometimes called him this:
A swine. For which she would not be forgiven
by the Russian poet. An English journalist,

Miss Hastings was an avante-gardist given
to aggressive views. The Paris
correspondent for *The New Age*, living

in Montmartre, it's said she'd had a tryst
with Katherine Mansfield. Legalized abortion
was her cause célèbre. A columnist

and editor—in fact we owe a portion
of the canon to her tireless service—
she "discovered" Ezra Pound. A course in

drama covering Shaw might footnote Beatrice.
And of course she slept with Modigliani.
We have pictures. She arrived in Paris

with the winds of war, by which time Anna
was embattled in St. Petersburg
and Modigliani, with a red bandana

'round his neck, was mixing wine with drugs.
He had a roommate at La Ruche, Soutine,
who had become perhaps his most absurd

obsession—"The finest work I've ever seen,"
he'd tell bemused associates. And when
Miss Hastings "fell" against the parlor screen

and kind of through a first-floor window, then
Modigliani's problem with the ladies
made the rounds.

                    "Let's look at that again."

Modigliani, in a heady state
of various dimensions, holds the nurse
up to the wall. "This painting I'd relate

to Rembrandt. You are working from the source,
Soutine. The grand tradition. With a twist."
Krémègne and Kikoïne, well, they've seen worse,

but Rembrandt? "Is there something that I missed?"
asks Pinchus. "Yes, but not by much. It's all
so … Russian! But this is Rembrandt. I insist!"

Outside, the sun dissolves into the pall
of 1916, halfway through a war.

    Is that the nude from MoMA on the wall?

Chapter 4

La Cité Falguière

I

888 Seventh Avenue, New York.
The famous "Opera Man", a semi-homeless
fixture, lifts his can and sets to work

another day, delivering his hopeless
arias. Removed across the Avenue
by uniforms at Carnegie Hall, the heartless

monsters, he resumes his ballyhoo
and de profundis on a sidewalk square
on 57th –just below the studio

of Ernest Crichlow on the second floor
of The Art Students League of New York.
Crichlow taught an open session there

on Thursday nights in '93. By luck,
I'd landed at an office right across the street,
above the "Brooklyn Diner." What the fuck,

I thought—the League! What better place to meet
the likes of Crichlow, Romare Bearden's partner
in the Cinque Gallery. And what could beat

three-hour sessions with the nude? Nirvana
every Thursday night. I'd cut across
the traffic snarled on 57th on a

blood quest with a bag of oil tubes tossed
and jostling on my back. It was a chance
to fail on par with painting in that most

auspicious gallery uptown. My pants
were caked with color on the night I met
a realist from the Harlem Renaissance!

"Another wild man!" Crichlow laughed. He'd vet
my canvas, shake his head, and say, "All right,
keep moving with the figure while it's wet."

When he retired, I switched to Wednesday night,
Harari's class upstairs. Hananiah,
he was full of love. In Europe at the height

of things, at home a "Socialist pariah"—
the blacklist and the whole shebang—this gentle
man was in his eighties. An American

who figured in the School of Paris! Judgmental
he was not, but all encouragement.
"I love this color," he would say, and bend to

see it closer in the battlement
of oil across my slab. "Spare no expense!
your métier's impasto!" There I spent

my Wednesday nights. An intense experience.
The weary model, having posed all day,
conveyed a softness. I would often sense

her weight and form through color in the way
that greens and violets would develop in
the pasty fleshtone I'd naively splay

across my gessoed canvas. I'd begin
to understand what Crichlow told me: "Work
it wet, and keep up with the drama in

the pose." Harari smiled—"I see a Turk!
An odalisque. Matisse would see the same."
The man was going blind. Sometimes he'd lurk

behind a student quietly, then—"What's your name?
You're Sally, right?" "Um, Robert." "Yes of course."
But he could see the paintings! When he came

to mine, I'd watch his eyes. There is a source
of clarity in art and in the process
of creating. And Harari had a vast resource

of images within. He could assess
a canvas with an acumen and skill
that cut through cataracts. "I'll tell you this—

you're learning how to work with white. It's still
the toughest color on *my* palette. Agh,
that's right. It's 'not a color'!" He would kill

with his derisive jabs at dilettante
opinions. I looked through catalogs and found
examples of his early work. His avant-

garde Parisian pictures brought to mind
Georges Braque. I came across a painting titled
Soutine's Studio. Soutine? Remind

me where I heard *that* name. In fact the wild
landscape that unsettled me at MoMA
was the start of something huge. Beguiled,

I studied Soutine on the train, at home,
at work—it bordered on obsession. So
I asked about it. "That one? My, oh my,

it brings back memories. Did you not know
I took his studio in Cagnes? He left
a week or two before I got there, though.

We never met." I have to say I loved
Harari all the more for this. "Where's yours?"
He'd lean into my painting. "It's improved!

Come back next week and give it three more hours."
And in the morning, there'd be Opera Man.
And I'd think, "You and me pal. Amateurs."

    *   *   *

II

La Cité Falguière in Montparnasse,
another bank of artists' studios,
takes over as our *locus dramatis*,

a setting for descriptive cameos
and narrative forays. Our subcommittee
of the Paris School moves into those

accommodations as we pass the gritty
domicile and cross the quay and river.
Paris truly is a walking city.

But, pardon me, is that an *Akhmatova?*
If it is, it has a uniformed escort ....
Modigliani's one-man show is over.

A public scandal, a police report,
fini. The best-laid plans of Berthe Weill
collapse into a kind of last resort

as her gallery becomes a Catherine wheel
of painters and police and painted women.
Léopold Zborowski cut the deal

to launch Modigliani with a one-man
exhibition at Weill's new venue
near the Opera ...: "Chaïm, I saw this coming,"

Pinchus claims. "Oh, really? Good for you.
But even I can handle simple math.
The Polizei across the Rue Taitbout,

a Modigliani nude enjoying half
of Berthe's window ...." "Still, it brought a crowd!"
"A crowd, it's true," says Chaïm. "It's moving fast!"

They each unhook a painting in the loud,
chaotic gallery and join the strange
parade. Modigliani is unbowed,

regrouping at a sympathetic change
of venue, Jean-Claude Arnaud's restaurant.
The artist, with his pictures and the flange

of sycophants that seems, these days, to haunt
him (and a crowd that tags along to watch),
advises, *"Give the people what they want!"*

Zborowski sighs and downs a double scotch.

Two hours ago, the comedy was at
the precinct house: "Madame, the painted crotch

on Rue Taitbout and all the others that
you show inside are filth. Paris abhors
such 'art.' It ends tonight, I'll see to that!"

"Monsieur Commissioner, some connoisseurs
might disagree," embattled Berthe
tries to reason with the bigot. "Yours

can hardly stand to represent the verdict
of a city. Besides, the Louvre is full of nudes."
"But, madame, yours show pubic hair!" (A word of

caution, painters—spare us, please, the rude
details). The laughter in the station puffs
the dull commissioner, whose attitude

is typical of any petty tough's.
His crowd is mobilized, and Berthe knows
the kind of work that crowds can do. "Enough's

enough," she whispers, and Zborowski knows
exactly what she means. He calls his team
to action. Word gets out and everybody goes

to Berthe Weill's to strike the show—Soutine,
Krémègne and Kikoïne, Chagall, Fujita,
working with the cops. A classic scene

prefiguring the work of Chico Marx. A bit of
Karl, as well, with painters and police
in solidarity. A works committee.

In the aftermath a gallery lease
is saved, if Modigliani's first and only
one-man show is scuttled. The gendarme seize

the moment, not the paintings—all the comely
canvases are stacked in Arnaud's closet
by the crew, whose eyes are on Zborowski.

"Now what?" Modi asks the dealer. Osip
Mandelbrot, the waiter, waits to hear ....
Zborowski lifts his glass and answers, "Road trip."

III

He wanted to get everybody out
of Paris, all his ragtag clientele
who'd emigrated from the roundabout,

La Ruche, to La Cité Falguière. "To hell
with everything!" Zborowski said. "The law,
the Cubists, and the galleries as well."

The bust at Berthe's was the final straw.
La Cité Falguière provided lots of space.
Some privacy—Modigliani saw

a real advantage there (he nonetheless
insisted that Soutine set up next door).
But with the proud Italian in disgrace,

Zborowski's "fresh air" stratagem seemed more
amenable to everyone. "For Chaïm,
I think Céret will open up a door,"

he tells Modigliani. "Frankly I'm
concerned about the fellow's perseverance
in a stuffy studio. It's time

he sees the Pyrenees. The kind of violence
he's attuned to, but in open landscape."
"I'm glad you've come around on Chaïm since

we last discussed his work. And an escape
from Paris wouldn't hurt Krémègne," replies
a tired Modigliani in his grape-

and hash-infused transcendence. "Léo, I
assume that Nice might also open doors." "Um, not
with the receipts from Berthe's." Modi sighs.

IV

Céret rolls over on a bed of flame
exposing an inflamed intestine turning
in upon itself. The slaughtered game

bird hanging over apples and a burning
candle on a table slips its noose.
An angled stairway cuts between the churning

mansard tiles and plaster walls. And who's
this man in profile praying? One of 12
engraved in gravity, a cracking sluice

of black and red and gold. Is he in hell
or heaven? Both! Courbet, Cezanne,
and Lautréamont. The vagaries of self-

denial. Obsession. There's that word again.
How else can one describe the opened door,
the breakthrough at Céret? How, other than

to show the paintings? Soutine is now at war,
endeavoring to cut the past, the shtetl,
from the pounding present on a tour

of Franco-Catalan elan and nettle.
Could anyone deny his cut at nature,
malleable violence at the metal

of the knife? Balletic. Gesturing in rapture.
Davening? My God, there's no escape.
At every turn, Soutine sets out to capture

everything, the color and the shape
of everything, destroying half his work
and burnishing a mountain with a scrape.

      Zborowski underwrote the bus that took
his coterie to paint the Pyrenees.
Fujita, as he'd hoped, brought a return.

The popularity of Japanese
design and Fuji's fusion with the West
meant steady business, selling from the easel.

Things moved rather slowly for the rest.
Modigliani made a rare attempt
at landscape. Interesting. Cezannesque.

Krémègne and Kikoïne were not exempt
from the nostalgia of Chagall. Their scenes
in village squares are fine. But the work of their

unkempt compatriot is grand. Soutine's
oeuvre coalesced. It piled up despite
the canvases he tore to smithereens.

Zborowski knew the market wouldn't bite.
But he had faith and Modi to remind him:
"Rembrandt wasn't Rembrandt overnight."

V

And nothing lasts forever. Now Chaïm is sitting
for a portrait. Modigliani's bellowing off-key.
The mock bravura here is altogether fitting.

"Let's do another one." "On what?" "Zborowski's
door!" "Oh no, Zborowski thinks I'm lousy."
"Nonsense. Léopold runs on-and-off.

He's like that. But he'd never count you out."
Modigliani tosses back his hair
and lifts the finished portrait of his mousey

protégé, the dealer's pied-à-terre
a ready studio now that Jeanne and baby
have moved in at la Cité Falguère.

And he's not kidding about the door—if maybe
about the dealer. Sketching Chaïm, he sings
an aria. He looks like he has rabies.

　　　　Jeanne Hébuterne was first among the things
that hit him like a truck on his return
to Paris. Star of his meanderings,

she caught his eye in Asnières-sur-Seine
one day, and that night on the Boulevard Raspail.
A modernist herself, Jeanne Hébuterne

was every inch the artist waif, a pale
and slender beauty with her hair
in plaited cords. An enigmatic Gael

with a beret. "Bonsoir, mademoiselle,"
he introduced himself. He was in love
the first time that he painted her (beware

obsession). And she painted him. She'd prove
a perfect soul mate for a shattered soul,
refined and self-abused. A portrait of

the tragic coupling: alabaster, kohl
(tuberculosis), amber. An alizarin
beneath the skein. She did not play the roll

of ingenue or *peintre maudit* in
the months that followed. She became his wife.
The mother of their child.
                    Obsidian

eyes alight upon the palette knife
and on Zborowski's door. "Soutine, she's pregnant."
"What? Again?" "We bring another life

into this world, Soutine. Another remnant
of our own." "But isn't one enough?"
Modigliani is disheveled, silent

as he works. He finally answers, "No."
Soutine, convinced his mentor's finally had it,
slumps. The months ahead are very rough,

the door of little consequence. "I'll add it
to the pile," Zborowski says the night
he kneels beside the deathbed of the addict.

Charcoal shadows in an amber light
attend the death of Amedeo Modigliani.
"Everything's in order, it's all right.

Berthe's taking several portraits, and I
have the rest secured. There's noting due ..."
"Léo. Thank you. Thanks for everything," he

answers. "And I leave everything to you."
There is no question he himself will vanish
with the dawn. Zborowski whispers, "What am I to do?"

"The work is finished. All that's passed between us
is accomplishment, for good or ill.
Beyond that, I will leave you with a genius."

Zborowski's eyes run over all the still-
wet canvases, Modigliani's last,
and settle on a door torn from his sill.

By Tuesday morning there's a death mask cast
in plaster and a wind-blown curtain through
which Jeanne, with child, a suicide, has passed.

Book
III

Chapter 1

The Depths

I

The port commission held a grand soiree
for business writers at the Marseille Bourse,
where Corsican singers filled a balcony

and the chandeliers went dark. Our final course
at dinner was the day-glowed architecture.
We sat and listened as we drank liqueurs

inside a lighted sketch of the prefecture
of finance circa 1899.
The Vieux Port lights intrigued us next, our

hotels beckoning across the water. Mine,
(Chopin's, and Popeye Doyle's) at harbor's head
cast chains of radiating light to shine

between the lolling sails. Marseille is bled
of light at the Phoenician port—beyond,
the boulevards go dark. In gold and red,

the city's lifeblood slips the gleaming pond
and finds the channel. Meanwhile, cracking Vespas
on the Rue de la République abscond

into the night. A tattooed junkie staggers
through the crawling traffic leaving town
to nonstop Euro sirens, shouts and whispers.

Later, on my hotel eiderdown,
I watch *The Lover*, Marguerite Duras'
idylle Indochine. A fallen gown,

the intermittent French, the golden lovers
bathed in amber, lodged in long bamboo
bring Marseille to a Champagne denouement.

And in the morning, Air Inter. The queue
for taxis at de Gaulle, a shapeless mass
of gray, proffers a silent *bienvenue*.

A cold October Saturday in Paris.
I hunker in the backseat of a car
that slugs through airport traffic past a Ferris

wheel in some forgotten lot before
it gains a thoroughfare toward the city.
It runs behind Montmartre. The Sacre Coeur

surmounts the plaster tenements. Its gritty
dome against the morning bed of clouds
recalls Marseille. Antique, bled-out, and shitty.

*   *   *

II

Modigliani's dead. And Gumilev
is shot by Bolsheviks in the absurd
cascade, as if one war were not enough.

In April, La Cité Falguière, interred
beneath the ashen skies of Montparnasse ,
maintains its furnace through a spring deferred.

Soutine, a keeper of the flame, will pass
another sleepless night and day at work.
His mentor gone, the atmosphere at Place

Émile-Antoine lacks energy. *Le cercle
de moderniste* spins aimlessly, off center.
So the painter labors in the dark,

his still life table charged with elemental
terror, dead things captured in the shock
of dying. Pheasants break their necks on tenter-

hooks and fish lie pleading in the stock
of nightmare. Bloody red tomatoes roll
on knotted tablecloths. An earthen crock

or tea pot lords the background where the soul
of an expiring ray casts quaking shade.
Chardin recast. Exhaustion takes its toll.

We see it also in the portraits made
on junk shop canvases. Tonight Paulette
Jourdain, Zborowski's secretary, stayed

for yet another sitting. Palette set,
Soutine begins. His pencil whirls across
the surface of a gessoed palimpsest.

The forms his laden brushes will emboss
emerge. And then the brushes lay a base
of earth tones, ochre, grays, a verdant moss

on which the gold and red are laid. A face.
The hands. A background, smoky Prussian blue.
Within the hour, he's working on the lace

around the collar of her blouse. "Are you
OK?" she asks. "You need to take a break."
"Don't move your lips," he says. "I'm almost through."

Paulette is trying hard to stay awake,
observing Soutine's face. His slackened jaw
conveys an openness one might mistake

for pure fatigue. She's seen this face before.
Modigliani also disappeared
into his reveries. Tonight, the floor,

a mess, is not conveniently prepared
for the repose that followed other sessions.
Chaïm, no Amedeo, seems almost scared

of intimacy. Paulette's first impressions
of Soutine were mixed if not confused.
He seemed naive and shrewd. A few confessions

slipped in conversation. He was abused,
he told her, by his brothers as a child.
He described his family as Russian Jews,

the poorest sort. He bounced between a wild
enthusiasm and a sullen silence
in the shortest conversation. Mild

but nearly menacing. No threat of violence,
but a vitriolic temper. What she thought he
needed was a woman's love. His reliance

on Modigliani notwithstanding, Soutine
obviously needed to be mothered.
He was sweet, if not particularly clean,

she thought. And even handsome, tethered
to his canvas by his shaggy brushes.
Paulette sees a gentle spirit smothered

under brutal circumstance. He touches
on her lower lip with pure alizarin.
He looks up at his model and he blushes.

"May I see it now?" "Of course you can,"
he smiles and lifts the painting from the easel.
He has daubed his name, that talisman

of blood, that blob of paraffin and diesel
flaming in the mound of corner loam
on finished pictures. Paulette finally sees the

image he's created. How, beneath the dome
of forehead, eyes of lavender and black
ignite a cobalt aura. How the plumb

of nose and mouth, the neck and torso track
a subtle S-curve. Paulette leans into
her portrait. There is suddenly a crack

and bustle on the stairs, a clomping shoe
outside the studio. "Police!" the artist
yelps. (*Á la recherché du temps perdu?*)

"Oh, Chaïm, it's only Léopold," Paulette is
still engaging with the picture. "Settle
down." Zborowski enters. "Are we finished?"

"Yes," Paulette says, seated on the metal
stool, becalmed and radiant before
her likeness and the phantom of the shtetl.

III

A cityscape awash in morning ash.
The aftermath of furtive glories burned,
the Place Émile-Antoine is strewn with trash

and overcoats and men who have returned
from war with ragged beards and broken shoes.
A league of beggared artisans concerned

with changing weather. With them sit the Jews
of Montparnasse, the painters of La Cité
Falguière. The boulevards and avenues

project this convocation, gray on gray,
into the afternoon, against a cloud
of dust around the boy from the café

and Chaïm. Their conversation's getting loud.
"You have to come, I paid you Saturday!"
Soutine is not particularly proud

in how he transacts business, one might say.
"I have to work tonight. I'll come tomorrow."
"No! Come with me now! Yes, right away,

Xavier. I'm almost done. I beg you, follow
me. Look here, I have a couple francs. I'll give
you three." Soutine prevails upon the callow

waiter. Our artist manages to live
on a paltry stipend from Zborowski, spending
more than half of it on models, a palliative

sum the dealer will recoup in pending
sales. The Russian meanwhile perseveres
in painting waiters, chefs, and housemaids, blending

apron-wearing servants into atmospheres
of pasted ash. Unhappily, the sinking
market guarantees a backlog. Fear

completes a circuit. Poverty, unblinking,
gains momentum as Léopold surveys
his store of portraits. We know what he is thinking ….

IV

The southern craterscape, where plaster hovels
lift their mansard rooftops, an infernal
floor, into the evergreens and gravel.

Nothing of the sun. The sky, eternal
earth tone in the quaking aftershock,
is sliding from the picture. A diurnal

nightmare, flailing forest, falling rock,
roll over slowly in a frozen wave.
Each picture captures chaos, taking stock

of where the future falls: an open grave.
Soutine spends 1921 and '22
in transit to and from the grand conclave

of Paris and the Pyrenees. A true,
long-suffering dealer, Léopold secures
a room and studio on Avenue

d'Espagne in Céret, a street inured
to shadows in its cage of Moloch trees.
The pictures come to Paris to be stored,

the pile-up hills and red catastrophes,
the Russian's tilted vision of the world
on fire. Soutine is almost on his knees

when Paulette comes in June. She is appalled
but not entirely surprised to find
him in a heap of junk shop paintings hurled

across the floor. He's scraped them to the rind
and painted them with gesso. "… Mademoiselle
Paulette," he beams. He rises from behind

a table spread with books and paraphernalia,
chunks of stony bread and drawings. "What
a mess, Soutine! *Mon Dieu!* Well, I can tell

you're busy. But you keep your windows shut?"
He's frozen for a moment, then he throws
his arms around her, crying. "Chaïm, don't

you ever read our letters? Everybody knows
you're working hard, but tell us you're alive
from time to time. Oh, listen, blow your nose."

"But you surprised me." "Well, I wrote that I'd arrive
this afternoon. But I'll stop scolding you."
"Sit down," he smiles, upsetting four or five

unfinished pictures on a portmanteau.
"I want to paint you just like this. Right now."

Zborowski balked when Paulette asked to go

alone for three days to Céret to find out how
Soutine was managing (his business kept
him on the boulevards that summer). "No."

"Why not? The hotel isn't bad. I've slept
in worse. And Madame Prèjean said she liked me
when we went in March." "You won't accept

no for an answer?" "It isn't very likely.
I don't have to anyway," she smiled.
"Well, Madame Prèjean's taken quite a liking

if she'll … let you stay for free?" "I'm not a child."
"Nor is Chaïm. In any case, I'll book
the room." Another debit filed.

Paulette was not prepared for how he'd look.
Despite Modigliani's self-destructive bent,
his influence kept Chaïm on the hook.

A leavening effect. But the money sent
down south this year has obviously gone
toward oil paints and canvas. And the rent.

"You look exhausted." Paulette, leaning on
the window sill, still seated on the case,
herself looks more than slightly travelworn.

"Let's get some air. You know, I think this place
is beautiful. Céret. And look outside,
I brought a friend. An interesting face

for you to draw some day." The black and bright-eyed
Sheeba, Madame Prèjean's cocker spaniel,
waits for them. And soon the dog's untied.

V

Krémègne accepts Zborowski's cigarette.
"Well, Pinchus, Berthe has agreed to take
your southern landscapes." "Does she pay?" "Not yet.

She takes them on consignment. For the sake
of argument, let's say she moves a piece.
We move in Kikoïne. Make no mistake,

We'll keep you in rotation. Berthe's lease
is covered. Modi sells …." "Of course. He's dead!"
"Of course. But what am I to do with these?"

77

His floor is literally carpeted
with landscapes from Céret. "… He doesn't sleep?"
"Paulette says no." Zborowski shakes his head.

Chapter 2

Madeleine

I

Paulette's account is accurate but light
on details. There are secrets she will keep
about the drama in Céret that night.

It was a matter of a good night's sleep,
a decent meal, a little mothering,
perhaps. A day exploring in those steep

environs might have come to anything–
Paulette invited Chaïm to her hotel.
The two had spent the evening smothering

the dog in roughhouse petting near a well
behind the studio. "Let's get some wine,"
Soutine suggested. "Promise not to tell

Zborowski." "Wine? But Chaïm …" "I'll be fine.
I know what I can handle." So it passed
that Paulette and the painter crossed the line.

In confidence, their friendship was recast,
and hours of conversation carried them
to bed. But that arrangement didn't last.

As Paulette got undressed, Soutine became
aloof. He sat beside her and his spirit darkened.
He pulled away from her, as if in shame.

Indeed, the situation somehow harkened
back to the vignette in Vilna, such
was Chaïm's uneasiness, and so it sharpened.

"Chaïm, are you all right?" "Oh, it's too much,"
he said. "It's just the wine," Paulette replied.
Soutine rocked back and forth in silence, couched

in agony beside her. When Paulette tried
to bring him back around—she stroked his hair,
she rubbed his back—he rose, and Paulette sighed.

The painter pulled a pillow to the floor
and tugged a blanket from an opened chest.
"I'm sick," he mumbled. Then he hit the door

like Dempsey hit Georges Carpentier. The best
Paulette could hope for was that Madame Prèjean
slept like lead. The undercover guest

flew down the hall. He made it to the john
and ambled back. Paulette was in her gown
by then and crafting him a couch to sleep upon.

"You cannot leave. It's late. You're sick. Lie down."
"Paulette, I'm sorry." "Chaïm, it doesn't matter.
You can have the bed or have your own

arrangement on the floor." He chose the latter
in embarrassment. Paulette knew how he felt
about her. Soutine was obviously shattered.

He stared up at the ceiling as she knelt
beside him on the floor and tucked the blanket
firm about his shoulder. "Well, good night."

And here we introduce a talking head,
Pinchus Krémègne: "In Vilna we would go
to brothels. The truth is that he couldn't get

a hard-on, not unless he had a throw
with something from the bottom of the pot.
My friend is shy. And working ladies, well, they know

his type. They're cruel. The nicer girls were not
an option. They humiliated Chaïm.
So he would skip that lot and take a cot

with the most wretched worker he could find
and shtup her like there's no tomorrow. Yes,
my friend could go the mile. He wasn't blind,

but I don't really think he saw the mess
he'd gotten himself into. And say a woman
interested him. He would obsess

about her. Trust me. But he wouldn't
even say hello. Not Chaïm. Instead he'd pay
to have some monster. Eh. We're only human."

Soutine looked up. He saw Paulette, the way
her nightgown draped upon her breasts.
He felt her body's warmth, but didn't say

a thing when Paulette kissed him. And the rest
is darkness.

               Soutine once looked up at the Chartres
Cathedral, at its bounding spires that attest

to Christianity's exclusive part,
the door to heaven, open just above
the clouds. Soutine felt set apart,

a Jew. "How could a girl like Paulette love
a man like me?" he thought. "Impossible."
He wasn't French. He wasn't good enough.

II

After all the Champagne and cigars,
despite the wine-dark snags across the loom,
beyond the night's cacophony of cars,

he wakes to whiteness and the same perfume
she'd touched along her legs on the divan
the night before. The woman fills the room

with a variety of beauties—her pecan
and velvet body charms the atmosphere.
Marcellin Castaing, a lucky man,

will wake this way for nearly fifty years.
There is a love whose purity defines
an age. An antique majesty. And theirs

is such a love, Marcellin's and Madeleine's.
Their privilege pales before sheer elegance
and generosity. Love so refines

the soul that even, if by happenstance,
the rich experience its harrowing
and finishing effect, the least pretense

of affluence evaporates. The arrowing
of stags, the piercing of the Cupidon's
artillery might illustrate a towering

maison and yet be more than decoration.
Her father was a famous engineer
in Chartres. He built the railroad station.

Marcellin, an art critic and heir
to some industrialist's fortune, twenty
years his lover's senior, kidnapped her.

His bride was seventeen. Elopement, he
preferred to call it. Jean-Claude Magistry,
the father of the bride, though reticent (he

hired a lawyer and a priest, initially,
to sue for an annulment), came around.
But the situation made for comedy.

Consider how the couple goes to town
at galleries. They purchased a Modigliani
nude at Berthe's once and sent it down

to Chartres to "impress" her parents. Any
hope for peace that weekend went awry
at dinner when the doorbell rang. Uncanny

how the poignant packages arrive
precisely at the point in conversation
where détente seems almost worth a try.

Marcellin unveiled the canvas. A sensation,
in the house of Magistry! "Have you no taste?
But it's preposterous. Marcellin, I question

your credentials as a critic!" Chaste
intent, the couple nonetheless defied
the father's protocols. "And what a waste

of money, Madeleine." The vilified
tableau now hangs above the antique bed,
that warm, imperial domain of white

at the château Marcellin inherited.
He rises, dons his satin robe and lights
a cigarette. "First thing?"—a tangled head

of hair emerges from the satin sheets
and smiles. "Come back to me, Marcel."
The woman lithely reaches up to swipe

his cigarette and takes a drag. "Ah, well … "
he says. He fishes out a fresh Gauloises.
and falls back on the pillows. "Darling, tell

me. Are you very angry?" "Me? What for?"
"The incident last night at the café."
"I'm not angry," says Marcellin. "I'm more

intrigued. But that was some display
of temper!" "Well, I hope he comes again."
"You do?" "I do. I heard Zborowski say

his landscapes hold a mirror to Cezanne.
He paints them in the Pyrenees. And Cagnes-
sur-Mer." "Well, he's a quite peculiar man."

III

Marcellin had called Soutine to la Rotonde
where he and Madeleine and certain friends
held sway—a kind of Saturday salon.

He'd heard about Soutine. And through the lens
of connoisseur and critic, with a far
more delicate perspective that depends

on intuition, he'd determined this bizarre
habitué of the Place Émile-Antoine
was worth a meeting. "I know who you are,"

Soutine replied. "… *d'accord*. Then we are on
for Saturday. And bring two paintings, please."
Castaing produced a card, and he was gone.

Two paintings. Soutine, his hands crossed on his knee,
sat talking to himself till after dark
with April's promise moving in the trees.

In fact it was Paulette who put the spark
to everything. She'd met Castaing at Léo's
and she told him of the painter in the park.

"Monsieur, you have to see his work. His heroes
are the masters. He is serious!"
Zborowski, busy adding up the zeros,

disapproved. "You are delirious,"
he told her later. "Sending Chaïm to la Rotonde?"
The dealer smiled with a mysterious

elan. "Paulette, I know you're very fond
of Chaïm. And I think this thing will end in tears.
But … there is *another* sailboat on the pond."

"Oh, first things first! Who knows how many years
your sailboat stays afloat?"

                              Our prospect jibes.
The night is full of stars! The moon appears

above the grand café, and now the tribes
of Montparnasse evaporate in shadow
giving way to those who will imbibe

the Champagnes and the Kir Royales. A halo,
jade and gold, enshrines the portico
of la Rotonde. Inside, Marcellin and Madeleine

lean close in conversation. "But you know,
Marcel, Soutine is likely to come late.
I'm sure he doesn't want to make a show

before the other painters." "So, we'll wait."
Madame Castaing proves prescient. She'd wondered
if he'd really bring his work to the ornate

café. She'd seen him often with a hundred
other vagrants on the stony Place
Émile-Antoine, pedestrians who thundered

madly in the evening traffic. Montparnasse
was still the squatter's park for avant-garde
bohemians, a thriving underclass.

But Madeleine saw how this man took it hard.
He'd carry pictures from his studio,
and through the crowd across the park, his art

seemed rather fine, if quite traditional,
amid whatever *isms* held the day.
He emanated from some protocol

of classic values in a cabaret
of wild reaction in her estimation.

"But I am *sure* I told him Saturday …"

The candles burn. In time, a calculation
of the evening's damages is slid
discreetly next to Marcellin's plate: An Appellation

Montpellier. A calvados …. "He said
he'd come." "But I think he's here!" Soutine,
a flea market fedora on his head,

is bounding through the room with Kikoïne
in tow and paintings—the portrait of a waiter,
a choking pheasant, and a village scene.

"Monsieur! Monsieur!" the flabbergasted *maître
d'café* pursues the two. "I see you've made it,
but you're very late. Sit down." "It's later

than you think," says Paul Guillaume, well sated
with the apple brandy as he looks the pictures
over. "I'm very happy that you waited

for me. I ... lost track of time. I picked this
portrait out especially ..." "Soutine,
I cannot see a thing." "Ridiculous!",

Guillaume exclaims. "Your eye's extremely keen,
Castaing. So, tell us what you think of these
extraordinary canvases." "We've seen

enough for one night, Paul. Now, Soutine,
I'm very interested, I must say.
But things are crazy here. Let's reconvene

tomorrow. At your studio? I'll pay
100 francs as an advance on any-
thing I buy. I think it's best this way."

He hands a clip of bills to Chaïm. "How many
here? A hundred? Take your money back!"
The clip is tossed upon the table. When he

goes dark, Soutine goes dark. And now a black
and bilious spirit fills the restaurant.
"If you had only bought a painting! [*wrack,*

disaster, oh faux pas!] I do not want
your money. What I want is your regard, Monsieur
Castaing." "Soutine!" Marcellin exclaims. "You can't

believe that under these conditions, at this hour,
anyone's prepared for doing business!
I will come tomorrow." Headed for the door,

Soutine yells back. "I would have been the happiest
man in France." Outside the door is Pinchus.
Kikoïne bows nervously. "Well, this is

slightly worse than usual," he thinks,
and follows. "Thank you both for your support,"
Soutine spits angrily. They cross the street. He sinks

into his overcoat. His grim escorts
are not inclined to understand. "You know,
there's something very wrong with you. He courts

you, and you throw him back his dough."
Krémègne goes on, "Everybody here
is starving, Chaïm. You could have struck a blow

for all of us. But you're impatient. Where
do you think you'll see that 100 francs
again? Zborowski's sinking. Don't you care?

You offend this guy, who's money in the bank,
and that cuts everybody out." "But *he*
offended *me*," Soutine returns. His blank

expression and his air of certainty
convince the other Russians that he's lost.
"I'll carry one of these," says Kikoïne.

"I don't even think my paintings cost
100 francs!" Soutine erupts. "I get
this money thrown at me. But then the boss

is too damn busy with his other guests
to see the work!"
                    "Soutine!" a woman
calls to him across the park. Paulette?

Or is he hearing things. "Soutine! There's someone
set to buy a lot of paintings! Léo's
up. He wants to see you right away. Come on!"

            *   *   *

IV

The taxi squeezes into Rue de Lille
as sunlight breaks the clouds. Musée d'Orsay
already has a queue. October's chill

and the grayscale airport drive give way
to leaded glass illumination as
the galleries light up for Saturday.

And I arrive at last. I check my bags
and walk around the corner to the Seine—
Café Voltaire, mahogany and brass,

croissant, café au lait, a sidewalk table. Then
I dodge the Vespas onto Pont Royal.
There is a side door to the Louvre—a friend

in Marseille claims it's how she beats the crawl
of tourists at the pyramid. But midway
on the bridge, I'm lost to Paris in the fall

in it's entirety. The Île de la Cité,
a shadow barge in autumn mist, divides
the trees, the ochre buildings on the quay.

Its spires ascend as Notre Dame collides
with cloud banks on the island's permanent
Elysium. A weathered tour boat glides

beneath the bridge toward a firmament
on the horizon. There is no time for the Louvre
today. I stroll the leafy arrondissement,

entering a plein air sculpture grove
along a path of yellow stone and cobalt
shade. The cumulus brigade above

dissolves into the grand cerulean vault.
Is that the Petit Palais on the right?
I know it has a major Georges Rouault!

Chapter 3

Snake Oil Man

I

The gentleman in the Harris houndstooth coat,
with the tortoiseshell glasses and pungent cigar,
is American, seemingly just off the boat.

The figure he cuts at Zborowski's is rather bizarre.
What follows, however, is one of our happier scenes—
A handshake. A deal! "Au revoir, Dr. Barnes." "Au revoir."

Thus our dealer bids bon voyage to *sixty* Soutines.
The Philadelphia man, who pays $3,000 dollars,
departs with his aide-de-camp in a hired limousine.

The paintings ship and a shake-up in fortune follows
as word gets out to the galleries and collectors.
Zborowski orders a little more starch in his collars,

and soon Soutine is absent among the specters
outside la Rotonde. He's seen wearing tailored suits
at clubs and the country home of his new protectors.

II

For background on this coup, we cross the cold
Atlantic Ocean and resume this song
in a place where quite a lot of things are sold.

In Philadelphia, a city that has long
administered a crippling social snub.
It's south of Boston. Still, if you don't belong

to certain circles round the redbrick hub
of Society Hill or Rittenhouse, you're in the cold.
Young Albert Barnes is poised to join the club

at Central High, the public school. He's told,
for boys like him, the university is out.
But Al, the butcher's son, is rather bold.

He studies chemistry, and finds a route
through Penn to Berlin, Germany. His call
to service not yet audible, he scouts

the standard pharmacopoeia and trawls
the molecules, a deaf ear to the skeptic
and competitor. He develops Argyrol,

a potent silver nitrate antiseptic,
good for gonorrhea, and brings it back
to Philadelphia, where things get hectic

at the pharmacies. He loses track
of all his invitations! So, he wins.
So, what? And what to do, now, with the stack

of bonds and dollars? Albert Barnes begins
to contemplate an art collection. Yes!
A great investment. William Glackens grins—

his old friend Barnes, a bona fide success,
will buy his paintings and, what's more,
deploy him as an agent, more or less,

in Paris, France, assigning him the chore
of scouting works of "modern art." At first
the agent hits La Butte de Montmartre to score

Impressionists. Renoirs—among his worst,
but some quite fine—Cezannes, Courbets, Degas.
And moving from the blesséd to the cursed,

he takes a taxi down to Montparnasse.
And there, he meets the dealers of Picasso
and Matisse. He's greeted with a general applause

and bags some masterpieces with his lasso—
Matisse's *Le Bonheur de Vivre*, the one
that caused the Spanish genius to scream, *"Asshole!*

I will steal his march!" thus kicking off a run
of masterworks and mean one-upsmanship.
Voilà! *Les Demoiselles d'Avignon!*

—(the girls give Philadelphia the slip,
but make it to New York). The envoy
makes it back to Dr. Barnes, his trip

recounted at the country club. "… A busboy,
or a waiter. No, a chef … a pastry cook!"
"He paints the worker! He is Russian. Like Tolstoy.

I'd like see his work." "I had a look
at some Soutines at Léopold Zborowski's …"
Dr. Barnes tees up his ball. "…It took

awhile to warm to all his off-key
tones. His figure paintings are off-kilter
and his landscapes tilt. He's very brusk. He's …"

"Russian!" Barnes exclaims and swings.
    The filter
through which Albert Barnes observes the world
is knit of class considerations. Quilter

93

and the quilt, he is replete among the manifold
downtrodden, such that armies up from sloth
invigorate his working class. A swirl

of immigrants adds texture to the cloth,
and Russians are particularly grand
in his regard. Preponderantly worth

society's esteem are those who stand
to gain the most in that they hold the least.
The doctor's not another Talleyrand

in Philadelphia—he shares the feast
on many fronts. A future trustee of
the premier school for blacks in the Northeast,

his mania for excellence and love
of education fosters opportunity.
He'll hang his paintings, one above another,

as an art school in his mansion. "Unity
of purpose, Glackens, fending off despair.
To Paris from the shtetl! That's community.

Some call it Communism. I don't care."
The argyled doctor speechifies until his small
white ball lands squarely on the green. "So there!"

Behold the man who parlayed Argyrol
into a "new aesthetic" open house
with two Soutines on almost every wall.

III

The Russian painter and his dealer, in cahoots,
set out to Cagnes-sur-Mer in style. They find
a decent studio and new pursuits.

94

The fights. The races. Once the deal is signed
with Barnes, Soutine emerges from the men
of Montparnasse and leaves that scene behind,

just as he once left Smilovichi. Again
he labors in the landscape of the South.
The air provides a steady antigen,

his art the constant antidote to sloth.
His lifestyle redesign is superficial.
In many ways, he still lives hand-to-mouth.

Essentially, he never leaves the shtetl.
He cannot stop creating. Seeing, drawing,
painting. Success will test an artist's mettle,

grace may lift his art above the warring
factions in the galleries, as friends
forgive or cross him out. A man withdrawing

to his work, responding to his vision, ends
his life on earth in paradise, alone.
Michel Kikoïne: "In fact, I will defend

Soutine. I'm not well-placed to throw a stone—
my house is glass. I'm but another artist.
We're a selfish lot. I have my own

regrets. Believe me. But I will say the hardest
thing to live with is a broken bond.
We aren't immune to feelings! I regard his

actions, starting with the Barnes deal and beyond,
as congruent with his unique obsession
as an artist and his *vue du monde*.

He paints and runs from poverty. Expression
and a disappearing act. He said goodbye
to family. He left his friends. But passion

can transcend the personal. It's why
we paint. It's *human* passion. People call it
a betrayal, but I understand this guy."

IV

Krémègne might disagree. He doesn't say.
Paulette would find some truth in Kikoïne's
perspective—she and Chaïm might well portray

the tragic confidants in classic scenes
of fate-distracted love and dedication.
She's a partner. She maintains Soutine's

connection to Modigliani, not to mention
his engagement with Zborowski, love
and sex the constant underlying tension,

art the topic at La Brasserie Bistrot—
"Madeleine Castaing expects you Sunday,"
Paulette beams. "And if I have to shove

you on the train, I will." Soutine's cache
of loose tobacco spills a little as he
rolls another cigarette. "You'll stay

with them again. That guesthouse on the grassy
glade!" "Of course I'll go. I'll bring a guest!"
He lifts a pint-sized glass of milk, his massy

lips embellishing a toothy smile. "You'd best
secure the studio down here till fall,"
Zborowski says. The tinny anapest

of Dixieland on the Victrola calls
to mind the music in the Ažuolas café.
"They want you for the summer, Chaïm. All

expenses paid." "They are likely going to *pay*
you for a few commissions," Paulette adds.
"You'll have no time to entertain!" "Ceréts,"

says Léopold. "Marcellin Castaing is mad
about the landscapes I've been showing him.
The ones that Barnes admired so much. I'm glad

he left a few." "Not me …." The painter's grim
expression now evokes Lugosi's Dracula,
prefiguring the monster at a milk glass rim.

"Too bad he didn't take the whole lot to America.
I want to scrape those canvases or cut
them up. Erase Céret!" "Don't get hysterical,

Soutine." "Chaïm, relax! They'll throw us out!"
His sidekick reaches over, takes his hand,
and stares him down. "Soutine, I have no doubt

the landscapes will find buyers." "But understand,
please, Léo. I've improved. I'm hammering
at landscape. And I've told you that I cannot stand

to look back at those rattling roofs and clamoring
catastrophes. Forget about those hills!"
"For Christ's sake, Chaïm, quit your yammering!

Don't *you* forget, those paintings pay the bills.
You signed them over, Chaïm. That's how it works.
I'm selling several to Castaing …."

V

                                    The mills.

The mountain hovels. All the sidelong jerks
and nightmare-stark positioning of trees
with clouds, the red stone walkways in berserk

striations, haunt the painters reveries
as he considers what he's done and where
his Cagnes experience has led: *Must these*

Céret monstrosities persist? And is it fair
to have them on the market if he feels
they mock him and reflect his mad despair

and everything he disavows? The wheels
of punishment. The shtetl and his bleeding
ulcer. Exile in the commonweals

of Paris and the southern village. Beating
back his torment in the fields of Cagnes-sur-Mer
the painter sees the broken hills receding.

Or is there something less dramatic here?
Might the lighter palette, open space,
and solid country houses under clear

blue skies in recent paintings show the face
of Côte d'Azure in contrast to the Pyrenees?
The artist paints from nature and a place

inside his soul. Let's first observe the trees.
Observe Cezanne. Compare Céret to Cagnes
in Soutine's painting. Evolving by degrees,

the painter's strong response to nature on
his rough-hewn canvases maintains a rude
integrity. A European one.

Tintoretto and El Greco, two
of the old masters who have long enthralled
Soutine, are conjured and imparted through

the earthquakes in Céret, their art recalled
in Midi sunlight on the humming fields
and ochre walls of Cagnes. A parasoled

pedestrian. A tripping wraith. It yields
a continuity and echoes forward
to the final landscapes where a forest shields

small children from a storm. He's running toward
a denouement, poetic clarity
along a country road. The lines are blurred.

Yet Soutine marks a sharp disparity.
He'll make his point with carving knives and boots,
destroying the Cérets. Barbarity

in studio and gallery. At La Bistrot,
Zborowski and Soutine are feral cats.
 "I've noticed, too, your interest in suits

and ties of late. Soutine, you're wearing spats!"
"We're twins! But I despise those twisted fruits,
those bastard landscapes …"
                              "Gentlemen. Your hats."

Chapter 4

Memorial Park

I

The summer lords it over Maplewood,
where echoes of the Erie Lackawanna
linger. Where the oak and maple stood,

where "Welcome" foliates a tailored lawn.
A remnant oak holds court before the station,
puffing in the blue suburban sauna

where the painter has no time for conversation.
Weingarten lifts his brush and wheels around—
"Not now." He braces in anticipation.

There are three acrylic landscapes on the ground,
the station and the oak on unstretched canvas.
"… Emil Nolde?" *"Go away!"*
                                              "Ah yes! The sound

of men at work!"—Here comes our Cezannesque
accomplice, Andrey Tamarchenko. "Rick,
you'd better take a few steps back! This man is

serious! He doesn't play." "The trick
is not to make comparisons, I guess."
"Not even to a Nolde!" "But it's so thick

and colorful. I love the way …." "Don't mess
with Paul. He's busy with his painting. Come."
Our Tamarchenko dabbles in noblesse

oblige, but he shines in empathy. The sum
of parts—a Russian Jew, an émigré,
a painter and a poet (via the ashram)

he's first of all a teacher. "I like the way
you've started here," he smiles as we approach
my easel, planted hard against the day,

a tripod in the grass. "Well, thank you coach."
"No, Rick, I think you've got a breakthrough here.
Don't fuck it up, OK? Don't get too much

into the detail yet. I'm over there
in case you need me." Andrey marches back
to where he's painting near the swale, his hair

and beard are animate in carbon black.
He sings, "By God, I think he gets it."
Perhaps I do, by God … perhaps I do at that ….

II

Andrey owned the Nandi Gallery,
a storefront school on Glen Ridge Avenue,
Montclair. The Sunday painters paid his salary.

He taught their children and employed a crew
of local painters who held classes and a camp.
The Nandi was an open studio

with an old tin ceiling and a standing lamp
that Andrey used to light his Russian models.
He was working on the nude. And he would stamp

each canvas with his signature, uncorking bottles,
cuing up Prokofiev, or Coltrane, or U2.
Gothic basilisks with painted wattles

glowered above his office door. Khatru
and Catherine. I'd visit late at night.
I'd come to paint on weekends, and we two

would hire a model for the afternoon. The light
that filtered through the frosted glass in front
washed everything in subtle grays, and white

took over every corner on the punt
of colors I'd establish on the bench.
We would both go at our canvas with a blunt

attack that subjugated drawing to the wrench
of gestural expression. But the form emerged.
Beholden to a raw technique, we'd drench

our canvases in tertiary hues. I splurged
on paint—that was the only reckless thing.
Andrey's cache of Veronese Madonnas surged,

impasto Titian beauties. He would sing
while painting. Petra from the harem of the Khan
would lie back, flushed and naked, listening.

And in the fall, he hosted a salon,
inviting friends and special guests like Tess,
a painter from Bayonne. We'd lounge upon

the oil-spackled couches and discuss
our calling. We'd critique each other's art.
Our tempers flared from time to time, of course.

"Tonight, the landscape. Paul, why don't you start?"
Our host dispensed the wine and moved the light.
Admiring the pictures was the easy part.

III

Paul Weingarten is an expressionist.
A painter out of time, a keeper of
the flame. He is a universalist

as well, distinguishing himself above
the times, and not behind, surrendering
to nature, motivated by a love

of beauty, and devoted to the rendering
of truth as he perceives it. And what is truth
but our perception? The humble tendering

of our experience, eternal youth,
forever probing the ineffable,
arriving at the solitary proof

of heart's response and the indelible
depiction of the soul. The light of God.
The vicious machination of the devil.

A personal mythology. Paul is odd.
An outlier by any Art World standard.
He is on his own, an avant-garde

insurgent battling in a gerrymandered
market. In a blighted century
he boldly held an out-of-fashion candle.

"It's all subjective objectivity,"
said Paul. "Da Vinci said it first, but hey!
The guy was paraphrasing Ptolemy!

The arts and sciences knew how to play
before the so-called Age of the Enlightened."
He painted scenes in series, like Monet.

The bridges and the power plants that frightened
and enthralled me on the turnpike as a child.
His still life paintings quiver with a heightened

sense of *nature morte*. The landscapes aren't wild,
but ominous and rich in color. Portraits
balance on the wire. He's reconciled

the features with the elegant or tortured
soul that speaks its name in Esperanto,
in the shadow play of human nature.

A picture is a chapter. It's a canto
in an epic poem. It stands alone
and sings in harmony above the mantle

with the forms in nature in a zone
of the ideal and the unreachable.
The cylinder, the sphere, the cube, the cone.

IV

"You're absolutely full of crap!" I said.
And Andrey stroked his beard: "So here we go!
Perhaps some more Chianti, Tess?" My head

was spinning. I tried, but I could not let go
of overpowering resentment. "OK.
'There *are* no lines in nature,' Paul, I know.

But somehow they showed up on the Passaic.
Your bridge, Paul! Line, … line, … line, … line.
I guess you found a *bridge* in *nature*." "Andrey,

I'm uncomfortable with this." "*Well, fine,*"
I yelled. "So why don't *you* get lost this time."
"Andrey, you can deal with Frankenstein.

I'm on my way."
        There wasn't any rhyme
or reason to the fit I threw. Insane!
But the crimson vale was visceral, the *Crime*

and Punishment routine. You cannot blame
a man for screaming till he's understood!
Or can you? It will never be the same,

I thought. I've cut Weingarten off for good.
But was he telling me to pack it in?
Perhaps it was the snub in Maplewood ....

"OK Rick. How did all of this begin?
asked Andrey. "Paul was kind of leaning on
your act. But the mentoring relationship's akin

to marriage, isn't it? Hey, Rick, c'mon.
You blew your stack. A typical Soutine!
And Paul is Paul. We'll all get over it. It's done."

I painted Andrey once. I laid a ring
of violet in an aura 'round his face.
And I can still hear Andrey Tamarchenko sing.

BOOK
IV

Chapter 1

The Model

I

Soutine left France, but only for three days.
One he spent before a painting at the Rijks-
museum. One—a Rembrandt with a baize-

on-red and gold motif. Ignoring the van Dykes
and the Vermeers, he stood all afternoon
before *The Jewish Bride*. He'd seen the likes

of nearly every other painting in the room
in Paris galleries. This one he knew
required him to travel—the wide balloon

of sleeve, the husband's hand, a field imbued
with subtle light conveyed in rich impasto.
No anecdotal narrative. The two

as one. A portrait of the newlyweds in cloth of
gold, a stole and crimson dress. The brooch.
The tenderness of physical and spiritual

union here personified. On first approach,
the painter realized the grandeur of
of the canvas. The grandeur of the oath,

the covenant, the coupling. *This is love.*
This painting is the apotheosis
of love. For all the glories in the Louvre,

no single work of art there lays so purely this
unvarnished, consecrated human space
before the heart. Beyond analysis,

this saying without saying. Hands and face
and gesture. No more is needed to convey
the human soul. This is all it takes.

The all-unreachable. He spent the day
conversing in the darkwood gallery with God.
Beholding Heaven. Being shown the way.

II

And in the field he had Courbet. Like any
painter mindful of tradition, Chaïm
made copies. But in a most peculiar way.

He hired country folk and farmers. "I'm
an artist and I'd like to paint you reading
on the grass. OK?" Before the Creeping Thyme

he'd copy from a reenactment, seeding
scenes with figures posed from the motif.
This method could involve a little pleading,

and often the vignette would come to grief.
"Soutine, I think the *other* one was willing,"
Marcellin complained behind the wheel. Relief

eluded him. "I need Marie!" "You're killing
me Soutine." They found her in the field
a mile away unoccupied and milling

in the hay. Soutine over the windshield:
"Marie! We're here. Let's get to work, it's late."
She lay down in the grass. Marcellin concealed

impatience. He let the artist concentrate
on his expressive version of Courbet's
girl reading in the sun. He'd have to wait

till after dark. "I'll need another day,"
Soutine, exhausted, mumbled on the ride
to Chartres. He'd scraped the woman's face away

and had to start again. He was denied
at first. His model's husband met the men
when they returned. "She promised!" "Well, she lied!"

"She has to finish! Do you know I pay her ten
francs every session! I paid this one ahead!"
"I refuse to let you paint my wife." "Well, then

you'll speak to my attorney," Soutine said.
He pointed to Castaing. "This painting's sold."
Soutine continued, "So it's on your head,

monsieur. I shall bring suit. Now you've been told!"
["*Mon Dieu*, Soutine, you'll land us both in jail!"]
"Take ten more fancs or pay 300." Rolled

and ready, Soutine's note, to some avail,
was held before the farmer, who accepted.
"Marie!" he called. He took the woman's pail

of golden apples to the barn and left it
to the artist to assume command.
"Marie, the book! I showed you how to hold it!"

III

But that was nothing in comparison
to Rembrandt's Hendrickje paddling in the stream.
Soutine employed a country matron and,

with Paulette's help, positioned her. She screamed
when Chaïm pulled up her gown to show her knee.
Again, he showed the Rembrandt to his squeam-

ish model. "Look. You're in the water, see?
You need to hold your gown above the water.
Just like this." The weeping willow tree

began to bluster, as Paulette established order
to the splashing scene. She calmed the model
but could not console the model's daughter,

who was crying on the bank. "The bottle!
Where's the bottle?!" "Madam! You must stand still!"
Soutine worked fast inside the winding throttle

of a rising storm. "My father will
be furious!" the woman hollered, certain,
now, the painter was insane, her shrill

report near lost along the rolling curtain
of the changing air. "Immoral! Yes,
that's what he'll say." She dropped her skirt in

whirling folds upon the stream. "Confess,
monsieur, this is a devilry, your art."
She grabbed the child and ran, her dress

snug on her ample thighs. A running chart
of colors on the canvas coalesced
as brushwork pulled the cloth and flesh apart

and clawed the skein. The rain began. A crest
of clouds caressed the blacking willow
as an atmospheric shroud appeared and pressed

around the figure swathed in nightgown billow.
"Chaïm! She's gone! It's raining really hard!"
He smiled wildly, twirling in the pillow

of the breast and belly. Paulette stood guard
against the canvas taking flight. "Oh, Chaïm!"
He flailed and scraped. He dallied on a shard

of shoulder—orange, blue along the rime
of flouncing neckline. Then he grabbed the painting,
ran it to the car, and just in time.

IV

The weather in the field. Soutine relied
on changes in the weather as he painted.
Forces felt within, that occupied

a landscape and a space that he created,
pressed against each other, merged and came
across as gusting forms. He never feinted

in his thrust at nature, endeavoring to frame
the model bending to a violent surge.
An inner light amounting to a flame

ignited sitters. Soutine, the demiurge,
drew subjects out of whirling chaos, held
them down, and hollered, when he had them, words

we've never heard but understand. He felt
his way. And violence yielded beauty, order,
sometimes calm. A summer rain might pelt

the canvas as he worked, but oil and water
stay their separate courses, parallel.
They never touch.
                In Paris, Soutine bought a

ray fish to reorchestrate the spell
of Chardin's Christ in agony. The red
tomatoes imaging stigmata, flowering hell

with sanguine pools. And rising from the dead,
the undead gliding fish. Its side is torn,
its viscera dangling just above a spread

of tablecloth in phthalo-shadow, worn
to tatters at the edge. A true Soutine,
Chardin's great ray is animate with thorn-

scraped wings against a field of green,
the color in the background of a portrait
Chaïm remembered at the Rembrandt stream—

a farm girl that he'd painted in a seated pose.
Her hands are heavy, folded on her lap.
Her eyes are like an animal's, like those

of something small and frightened in a trap.
A rabbit or a squirrel. A simple country girl.
And Chardin's ray. The wet tomato sap,

the oils and fish rot mix as we recall
the painter's struggle on the rainy stream.
For here are still life objects in a squall

of rearrangement. Fish and table seem
to totter toward a fall. The priapistic
spoon and heavy jug that frame the dream

manipulated, in a near sadistic
pummeling of battered brush and hand,
convey a frightening, expressionistic

anguish. This is Calvary across a strand
of sideboard. This is agony and rapture.
And all that Soutine wrestles with is banned—

the food, the wine. The artist tries to capture
a forbidden, alien tradition,
one that terrifies, to give it structure

and submit to it in fear of extradition
to the ghetto, to the Russian shtetl.
Entrée. An ironic joke. A frisson

and a fear combined. The taste of metal
dominates his still lifes of the ham,
the turkey, and the ray above the kettle,

Christianity no nearer than Islam.
Still, nothing is so sorely out of reach
as that eternal pair in Amsterdam.

Chapter 2

The Carcass of Beef

I

Madeleine Castaing commissioned Chaïm
to paint a portrait of Madame Giroux.
She told her husband, "I'm aware that I'm

surrendering a day to looking through
the galleries for two Cérets." He smiled.
They found the ransom. Luckily the two

available were palette scrapings, wild
and hardly realized. Reluctantly
they turned them in, and Chaïm reviled

them with a hammer claw. The blasted tree
and slanted mansard roof were badly shattered
by the time he finished. The beating lasted three

or four ungodly minutes! Torn and tattered
canvas at his spattered boots, the painter
gasped in extremis, as if he'd murdered

them. His faithful patron waited, her
chapeau secured beneath her chin
with fine elastic, in the corridor,

her nervous smile struck brilliant red and thin.
The sounds she'd heard had registered as sex
crime. "Oh, Madeleine! I'm ready to begin!"

called Chaïm. "Madame Giroux will come at 6,
as planned, Soutine. May I come in?" He showed
her where he'd draped the chair in rich

sateen, a swath she'd given him to throw
beneath the sitter. In all respects, the space
was *trés* bohemian. Madame Giroux
would certainly approve.

The picture chase,
Soutine's requirement that Madeleine
deliver two Cérets (which he'd debase)

for every one he painted on commission,
put the early landscapes on the firing line.
But the survivors in the Barnes collection

can attest to how, like Victor Frankenstein,
the fledgling painter came to terms with nature
at Céret. A mirror on Soutine,

they hint at how he could not face the monster
he'd created. How the monster followed him
to Cagnes. *Those* landscapes hang in Pennsylvania

with the pastry cook, between the grim
portrayals of the Pyrenees in France.
Chateaux and cataracts, the wind, a slim

suggestion of the human form askance,
transcend stylistic nuances and shifts.
The scene—the raw dissemblance in the danc-

ing trees, the plunging line of sight that lifts
the mountains to erase the smoking sky—
is tamed in Cagnes but loses none of its

eclectic edge. The vagaries of eye-
to-hand reflect the landscape of his heart,
his shtetl soul. Soutine has no alibi.

Madame Giroux arrived. She played the part
of grande dame in a hat that hardly fit
the canvas. And Soutine worked like Bonaparte,

hell-driven, coming to a composite
of farm girl, ray, and roofscape in Céret.
A roiling S, a wave in royal red.

II

They'd broken through the old brick wall in Castaing's
carriage house, a renovation under way.
Soutine took full advantage of this, casting

chickens in full plumage pendent, gray
and gold and green against a jagged frame
of darkness, squawking in the ecstasy

of death. Talons, beaks and wattles flamed
and sputtered in a nightmare space of murder
on his canvas. A still life series ran to game,

the hare against the green slats of a shutter,
the turkey on a cloth with golden apples.
Soutine conveyed their extremis in color.

Not satisfied, he bartered with his hapless
dealer to procure a side of beef
when he returned to Paris. Butchers grappled

with a battered carcass up the stairs, a brief
comedic interlude at the apartment
he'd been renting. To the hired men's relief

it made it through the door. The painter sent
for Paulette once the butcher's boy had hung
the cage of ribs. His motif was the Rembrandt

118

at the Louvre, that bleeding carcass strung
upon the rack across a room ... the girl
appearing at the door. But Chaïm would come

a little closer to his model. And he'd hurl
himself at more extensive spans of canvas.
Paulette arrived to find him in a world

of meat, his palette fat with gristle and his
model dripping on the floor. She placed
a pan to catch the blood. "But Chaïm, can this

thing hang here overnight?" Paulette could taste
the painting as the smell of colors mixed
with beef. Apparently the painter faced

another sleepless night. His helper fixed
herself a bed this time, but had to wake
each hour to baste the hulk. "Paulette, the trick's

to keep it bleeding," Chaïm commanded. "Make
it wet." She wetted it. And when the morning sun
came shining through the window, you'd mistake

the carcass for a red Céret, a run-
ning track of bones beneath a sagging skein.
By noon, the horrid greenback flies had come

and Soutine had another canvas pinned
and propped against an oil-splattered table.
He mixed a pile of cobalt and alizarin,

a blackout violet at the center of a scumbled
wheel of colors bleeding into gray.
His oil palimpsest began to bubble

119

in the heat as Soutine layered splay
on splay of tortured meat between
the scratchwork ribs to end the second day.

And sunrise found him scraping back the green
he'd laid in semidarkness. Hours passed.
The colors changed. The carcass wore a sheen

of viscous rot, its rind a venous blast
of atrophy. It cracked in hieroglyphs
of morbid skin. The painter, slouching, cast

his shadow on the sagging monolith.
By 12 o'clock, the neighbors were amassing
in the hall. No one ever bothered with

Soutine from day to day, but he was asking
for it this time. The building smelled like rotting flesh.
The landlord pounded on the door. "You bastard!"

"Go away!" "Enough, Soutine. Unless
you haul that garbage from the building
I will have *you* hauled away." This fresh

affront made Chaïm throw down the brush. "You're killing
me! I told you fifty times—*I paint!*
This is my studio." The landlord was unwilling

to put up with it, and a complaint
was filed. The gendarmes were the next to knock.
"Soutine, you have to let them in." This faint,

exhausted plea from Paulette hit him like a rock.
He stopped his painting, calmly turned around,
unlocked the door, and opened it. The shock

was registered succinctly when the gendarme found
the carcass hanging in a buzz of flies.
"Explain, monsieur." The captain looked around

as Soutine plied him with apologies
and Paulette fumbled with the swatting broom.
He saw the three completed pictures. "These

are marvelous," he mumbled, and the room
depressurized. The sympathetic officer
allowed the tired painter to assume

the mantle of an artist in the aperture
of his protected space. No law applied.
"I agree you should continue here, monsieur,

but how securely have you got this tied?"
He checked the knots and nodded in approval.
"Are you familiar with formaldehyde?"

He suggested opening a window. The removal
of the body was postponed until the weekend,
giving Soutine three more days. In all

that time, Paulette would later swear, her friend
remained awake and working. They hardly spoke.
Soutine, his shoulders hunched, would lean against

a chair and load a brush and lunge. He broke
a dozen brushes in a day. Three times
he tried to eat—but eating made him choke.

Paulette would pull the bowl away. "Oh, Chaïm,
you need to stop." "I'll finish when
it falls apart." It fell. And from the slime

his hanging carcass series rose to 10,
each painting fully spread with crucified
and falling cattle, seething gristle end-

to-end. On Saturday, the thing would slide
across the floor and down the stairs and out,
a golem slab extinguished in a tide

of passion, fallen in a savage bout
of extra rounds. Soutine himself collapsed.
Zborowski paid to sanitize the rout

and crossed the landlord's palm. Paulette, perhaps
intuiting an impact on the painter's
ulcer, diagnosed exhaustion as a relapse—

she'd seen him through the throes of stomach pain.
Her premonition, her experience,
and her devotion would serve him well again.

III

The painter's fever dream is borrowed from
Hieronymus. An animated field,
a Christian allegory in the scrum

of man and crow. A seventh seal unsealed,
the belly of a Vilna prostitute,
embodying the world, is slit and peeled

a gaping valve, a gulping dread, a chute
that suckles hybrid animals and trees
beside a bloody lake of leaking fruit.

Soutine, the pilgrim, struggles on his knees
astride a silver pickerel or pike
that grins and gambols, retching on the sleaze

and burping on the slime it swallows in the strike
and wallow through a riotous regalia.
A robin's head atop the whore shouts, *Kike!*

and beaks a heart on which is carved "*Regina
Angelorum*" … *Kike!* …. Angelic hands
administer a salve that trickles from a kind of

ladle on the sliding field, the strand
of aching scales, the open bowel of venom.
Now the angel, or a novice nun, dabs gland

and gash with something like an amber vellum.
Words appear, familiar but unread-
able. Romanian. The dreamer's hell on

velvet slides beneath the sun, against the bleed
of everything and nothing to a path
through forest where he meets his guide,

an eight-foot sparrow with a birch stick lashed
against his leg. By way of introduction:
"*Mon nom est Marc. Je suis aussi un Juif.*"

The dreamer follows Marc by means of suction
on his rutting fish. The trail is mostly mud,
the forest evergreen. A red eruption

pulses to a heavy sonic thud,
a flare at the horizon's verdant peak.
It is a fire from the dark volcanic heart

that's harrowed at the curséd robin's beak,
its slur a cracking echo in the forest …
Kike! …. The sparrow turns again to speak.

"Verboten!"
      The word rings dreamlike, strange, divorced
from reason (*Warum nicht auf Deutsch?*) as Marc
stares ardently, expecting a response.

The gulping mudslide pike is now a stark
embattlement of bones. Soutine, asunder,
wades beside a prehistoric shark.

A shovelhead. He hears the sound of thunder
as the mud runs crimson, covering his arms.
The sparrow grabs him just as he goes under,

folding him beneath a wing. Alarms
are sounding. Cannons roar. The robin shrieks
against the lightning, and the sparrow's charge

is pressed between its bosom and its beak—
the bird attempts a feeding.
                              Kike! ...
                                    "Verboten!"
Overhead the sky congeals, a rack of beef.

Soutine, unfolded from the wing, beholden
to the sparrow, stands before a prelate
of the Church of Rome, a pope enthroned

between the curtains of a bleeding slate
of ribs and rotting meat. The pontiff screams,
his neck in knots, his dentures like a gate,

"God, do it with the knife!" Our sparrow cleans
its feathers with a flourish of its beak.
The pope is crying and the dreamer dreams

into the velvet slide, the steady leak,
the bosom of the brown, maternal sparrow
as it glides across a burning lake.

The pilgrim, pressed against the throbbing marrow
of the angel heart, no longer hears
the canon of the man of constant sorrow,

but only wafting birdsong fills his ears
for as the barking pontiff pleads for death,
the breasted bird dissolves in mourning tears.

Soutine, resurfacing, is conscious, short of breath
but breathing. "Chaïm, are you awake? Your fever
broke." Paulette is kneeling at the River Lethe.

The battles in the week gone by, his labor
and his ecstasy, come back to him
beneath the rig he improvised, the lever

used to lift and hang the beef. It bears a grim
resemblance to a gallows in repair.
He senses twilight, following the rim

of sun along the largest painting there.
The pendant rind. A Peter crucified.
He breathes and runs his fingers through his hair.

Chapter 3

Show Time

I

Paris, nine years after war, was still
a locus for the arts. The coterie
of innovators from the chalky mill,

established as the new academy
(the destiny of any avant-garde),
invested in chateaux in the Midi.

But Soutine summered in his patrons' yard
in Chartres and rented space in Montparnasse,
a studio apartment near the Boulevard

Pasteur. Wearing his fedora, he wandered past
the plazas and the parks where he once sat.
Krémègne and Kikoïne had left the Place

Émile-Antoine behind. They'd sometimes chat
with Chaïm in the cafés. They had careers,
a cut above the proletariat.

And Léopold Zborowski, in arrears
or barely breaking even, sold the Russians'
work. He'd seen them all through brutal years,

but things were looking up—there were discussions
of a one-man show for Soutine at the Bing,
a gallery that showed van Gogh, and a hush in

the Café Les Fleurs du Mal, enabling
the businessman to manage expectations:
"Siegfried Bing came back. He's offering

September, Chaïm. The perfect month—vacations
over, buyers into their routines
and back to business. And there are indications

of a very active fall this year." But Soutine's
hearing was selective. "*Wait* a minute.
I thought his name was *Samuel*." "A means

of doing business Chaïm. *Siegfried* isn't
French, in fact it's German! *Nichts zu gut,
mein freund.* There's not a lot of money in it."

"Is he a Jew?" "I didn't ask him, but
I doubt it ... anyway. The carcasses
should be the centerpiece. We'll put a cut

of sirloin in the window. In part, this is
a show of still lifes, Chaïm. Your recent work."
"But if he's Jewish ..." "... then he never practices.

For God's sake, Soutine, drop it! OK, look.
You're going to meet a lot of people there.
It's inappropriate, indulging in this quirk!"

"But we should talk." "We're talking, Chaïm. I'm here!"
"*Negotiate.*" "With Bing? We're in the door
already!" "No. With you and me." "Oh dear."

"I don't like 50/50 anymore."
"We'll work it out, Soutine. We'll work it out."
The painter shrugged. "Zborowski, don't ignore

me." "What? I booked you at the Bing! I doubt
Guillaume gets painters near the place, my friend.
And it isn't like I've got a lot of clout.

I stuck my neck out for you once again.
Ignore you. This is what I mean. You make
no sense!" "So how 'bout 40/60 then?"

"We'll talk."
                         Not talking *then* was a mistake.
They each had their legitimate concerns.
A show at Bing's could arguably take

in more than either of the partners earned
in any "normal" year—a normal year
consisting of the gallery returns

for Léopold, whatever he could clear
with his collectors, and commissions for
Soutine. Paulette Jourdain was the cashier.

Any proceeds from a sale in which Zbor-
owski brought the buyer came in 50/50.
When Madeleine Castaing was guarantor,

all money went to Chaïm. Nothing shifty
in Zborowski's dealings, everything transparent.
But an exhibition at the Bing could lift the

curtain on a pantomime of errant
possibilities—especially for Chaïm.
The upside for Zborowski? Less apparent.

For the dealer, who'd invested time
and money to support the struggling Russians—
himself existing on the edge of crime

and punishment without a lot of cushion—
the Bing could mean a payback, all in one.
But Léo undermined negotiations,

when he could, by saying that he had to run.
He put the painter off. And thus, the Bing
would mark a turning point for everyone.

II

The valet that he'd met at Maxim's sat
for Chaïm in his Paris studio. A lot
of cadmiums were mixed and layered fat

to clothe the worker in a bloody clot.
The doorman was gregarious. He told
Soutine about his childhood—it was not

particularly interesting. Same old
same old, as they say in France, except
the part about the vestry in the cold

cathedral. Soutine, who truly was inept
at small talk while he painted, finally spoke.
"You were a choirboy? Do they accept

a kid in your condition?" "What a joke!"
the valet answered. "*All* of us were poor,
believe me. And they work you once the yoke

is on." Soutine was interested more
in what he wore. "I guess I've always worked
in uniform. And now I work the door

dressed like the devil." The valet laughed and jerked
his head in doing so. "Sit still, I'm nearly
done." Soutine knifed color on a torqued,

extended arm, the palm turned upward, clearly
trawling for a tip. By ten, he'd wiped
his brushes with a rag and paid his squirrelly

sitter. And when the man was gone, he swiped
a red "Soutine" across the carbon black
at lower right.

              Madame Castaing, in a striped
ensemble with her famous chin-strapped hat,
smiled broadly when she introduced the painter
to the curate on the lawn outside the shack

he called his summer studio. She'd explained her
Russian friend's peculiar interest and request.
"Our Madeleine speaks highly of your work, monsieur."

Soutine shook the soft hand of the priest.
"We'd love for you to join us in an hour for lunch,"
the hostess winked. Soutine put on a vest

and jacket, slicked his hair and picked a bunch
of wildflowers from behind the studio–
some color for the table, though the punch

Madame Castaing brought to the patio
became the centerpiece. A garden repast
with a Catholic priest, Commedia

dell'Arte on the menu. Chaïm is cast
as the artistic intellectual,
supported by his manners and his bast-

ard French. Madame Castaing, per usual,
gives us Ariadne, facilitator in
the verdant garden, wise and beautiful.

The parish priest is Father Tatarin.
"Today, I walked the father through my whole
collection." "I'm impressed, Monsieur Soutine.

I'm fascinated by the Russian soul."
"The feeling's mutual," the painter smiled
irreverently above his china bowl

of chicken broth, a lunch that mixed the mild
with the familiar-if-a-tad-cliché.
"Father Tatarin admired the child

and mother." "And those scenes in Italy.
Or is it Spain? You know, the frightening hills!"
Soutine shot daggers at his hostess. "A Chablis

for Father Tatarin, Marie, and water, still,
for our illustrious Monsieur Soutine."
Madame Castaing possessed a special skill

in calming Chaïm. But her laughter said: I win!
"Madame tells me you would like to paint
the choir at Chartres Cathedral. Madeleine,

it is a wonderful idea!" "Wait! Wait!"
the painter said, and raised his slender hand,
"I only want a boy or two to sit

for portraits in their capes." Father Tatarin,
sat straight, perplexed. "A boy or two in capes?
I'm afraid, monsieur, I do not understand."

The hostess rolled her eyes and passed the grapes
to her confused curate. "The choir gowns.
Those luscious frilly gowns. Strawberry crepes

they are. So red and white. Those little frowns
and folded hands—I see a row of portraits
now!" she beamed. The awkward painter downed

a glass of water. "Portraits," said the priest. "Is it
portraits like the mother that you want
to paint? But why the choir?" "Well, of course, his

forte is the portrait series, …" "And I can't
paint at the church," the painter interrupted.
"… He likes the gowns," the hostess smiled. "Their saintly

dispositions. They're so sweet." "And uncorrupted,"
the priest imparted to some glancing ghost
or an imagined friend. An inside quip?

"Yes. Well, Marcellin and I should host
the sessions. Chaïm will paint them in our home."
A premonition the commission might be lost

advanced as Father Tatarin peered from the dome
of his enormous head at Chaïm. "It's strange,
Monsieur Soutine, that the Church of Rome

has such appeal. A bit outside the range
of your yeshiva boys, our choir. I'd guess
there'd be a comparable mélange

among the Jews of Paris, many of whom dress
in capes and cowls and such." "Father Tatarin,
I hope you'll let me paint the boys." With this,

Soutine rose up and walked across the lawn.
The priest, laconically, observed his exit
fingering his glass. "Don't get me wrong,

Madame. I'd like him to proceed. It's just that …
parents get involved. And the Monseigneur."
"Marie! get father Tatarin his hat."

"Oh Madeleine, please understand, you're
asking for these boys to sit, alone …"
"They will be here with us. And be assured

each sitter's family will be paid. We're known
to be quite liberal in a Catholic cause or two.
These paintings, we believe, would rank as one,

no matter if the painter *is* a Jew.
Marie!" "Now, Madeleine, I understand.
I'll speak with the Monseigneur and I promise you

I'll square it with the choirmaster *and*
Soutine. Perhaps by Saturday." "I trust you
shall." She shook the curate's sweaty hand.

III

The famous Bing *a la rentrée.*
Picasso's there. He wears a floppy hat
as a disguise (a total giveaway).

And there's Guillaume, the famous dealer. Fat
and fussy, dressed in black with pasted hair
and subtle touches of the caliphate

of high finance, the connoisseurs appear
and slowly acclimate beneath the wings
of Soutine's rays. A painted abattoir

emerges from abstraction. Garish things
claim shadow space. A shock of recognition
runs the room—the maid in apron strings,

the side of beef, a flowing transposition
from the flailing cock against the bricks
to white chateaux and classic composition.

Guillaume believes his eyes are playing tricks.
Remember Rembrandt? This picture's a Courbet!
It seems as if this man Soutine could fix

chaotic nature, make it sit and stay
and shudder as it breathes a final breath.
The hemlock rows behind the houses sway

beside a hanging pheasant in the throes of death.
Picasso couldn't stay. He said goodnight
and half a dozen cubist painters left.

Madame Castaing, arriving in a tight
Chanel ensemble, glides with Marcellin
across the gallery, her smile, all white

and red, cuts brightly through the clientele.
"Krémègne!" she waves to catch the painter's eye.
"Good evening, Madeleine, you're looking well!"

"Marcellin remarked as we arrived the sly
arrangement in the window. Very like
a flesh and blood cathedral. A sacristy

of bones and meat. Parishioners are pike
and wild turkey in their apple pews."
"It's everybody's funeral. Don't strike

a match—formaldehyde," Krémègne's enthu-
siastic comeback. "Here you have it then.
The blood and bone cathedral of the Jews!"

"Mon Dieu! Do *not* tell Father Tatarin!"
She pecks the artist's cheek. In fact, the priest
moves through this crowd, another man

in black unsettled at the painted feast.
Paulette and Léo entertain Guillaume
as Father Tatarin goes beast to beast.

Soutine, in perfect form, refused to come,
despising connoisseurs' congratulations.
Michel asks Pinchus what they'd think back home,

"The mohel would find it somewhat ostentatious,"
says Krémègne. "But he might be jealous of the pike."
"He really is a putz on these occasions."

Meanwhile, Madeleine is moving like
the hostess at a party, showing friends
the pictures. "My husband, Marco, used to hike

near Cagnes-sur-Mer," says Madame Geoffroy-Lenz.
"I know this country house!" "He's done a series.
And we own a couple." Madeleine extends

an invitation, fielding several queries
from Madame Giroux, who interrupts
the conversation. "Ah! Monsieur Gutierrez …!"

Madeleine moves on. "I've had enough,"
Zborowski grumbles, as he gulps his wine.
"Is that woman selling paintings?" "For the love

of God, Zborowski. That's just Madeleine.
She's being Madeleine," Guillaume intones.
"Of course she is," Paulette agrees. "It's fine."

It's fine. The gallery of blood and bones.
The Calvary of cattle hunkering.
Devoid of cylinders, and spheres and cones,

devoid of cubes, the brilliant Bing
recalls the streets of Vilna and the dirty road
to Minsk. A destiny of wandering,

a want of love, of family, of home.
A choirboy looks down upon the gathering.
Within the hour, it's purchased by Guillaume.

Chapter 4

Our Fathers

I

Andrey's basilisks, unscrewed, lay stacked
and tied beneath a painting of the fire
and another of a clan along the tracks

at Watchung Station. Images of dire
circumstance, the fallout from Ground Zero
smoking fifteen miles east, aspire

to visions of deliverance. No hero
in a uniform with 80 pounds
of gear, no politician playing Nero

in a Georgian bunker, but families drawn in browns
and grays against a sky of searing red.
In one, a naked mother hands her baby down

to open arms, a bearded man, his head
below the fault line of a blasted landscape. He
is recognizably the artist. Lead

flows gold and molten post-catastrophe.
The other painting—is it called *Departure?*—
brings to mind Zhivago. Nandi Gallery

is dark but for a blue light from the aperture
of office door and the streetlight's halide glow.
The movers come tomorrow. "Is that your

painting on the easel, Rick? Cuz everything must go!"
The Russian bellows from his sanctum sanctorum.
He heard me at the door—Tamarchenko

always heard me coming. "No. But some
of these against the ledge are mine I think."
"OK, but tell me, whose the hell is *this* one?"

Coming from the office, leaning on the sink,
he indicates the painting on the easel.
"I don't know." "I think I need a drink."

The studio is packed for Ellenville,
New York, where Andrey and his family
have access to a farmhouse. Did the evil

season prompt this change? Or is the émigré
metabolism such that settling down
is not an option? Andrey will not say.

I ask him, but he does a dance around
the subject. "Yes, I know, it's risky, but …"
"We'll miss you in Montclair." "I'll miss the town.

Look, this is how I roll," he laughs. "I cut
and run!" "Has Paul been by?" "Um … yesterday.
I've got some wine. We're out of Guinness stout."

We spend an hour talking. Saying goodbye.
He shows me paintings that he's done upstate—
a group of winterscapes. "I really like the sky

in this one. Sunrise?" "Set. You like to skate?
We have a pond. You should come up and paint."
"I will," I say (I never would). "It's late.

I love you, brother. Best of luck." "But wait!"
he hollers. "…Whose the hell is this?"—the painting
on the easel, a flower bed by a garden gate.

*   *   *

II

The crash of '29 knocked Europe over
like a house of cards and set the stage
for war. The history we know. We know the

horror of the years ahead. But a page
may yet be written to illuminate
a smaller drama. A history to assuage

a sideline curiosity or sate
an interest in some personal affair.
For history tells us stories small and great

of those who ran away or stayed. Of their
peculiar traumas, tragedies of love
or family or business. All despair,

demise, and triumph matters. The story of
the dealer Léopold Zborowski is a case
in point—the details of his dropping off

the canvas. That thin and tired, bearded face
Modigliani painted is prophetic.
A gambling amateur, he'd earned a place

among the dealers in Montmartre. Aesthetic
taste, his clientele of Russian prodigies,
his calculated risks—with a pathetic

setback here and there but few apologies—
amassed for him a sizable account.
But Léopold's investment strategies

were questionable. He drank a good amount.
And he lost Soutine, the ace that Amedeo
dealt him on a deathbed. Winds in Mont-

parnasse had shifted. A perceived betrayal
rolled and rollicked in the galleries,
cafés, salons, and boulevards. A stale

resentment blossomed in the dealer's arteries
as big collectors bartered with the Bing
for access to Soutine. The Tuileries

survived three winters, but the flailing spring
of 1932 left Léopold
depleted. And the summer, faltering

toward World War II, a grayscale season, cold
and spare, would find Zborowski gone.
A paupered angel in a heaven sold

to highest bidders, Léopold passed on
in anonymity, an also-ran
footnoted in the sprawling marathon

of modernism. A peculiar man.
Undone in his devotion to the cursed,
he served the outcome of a higher plan.

III

The curse continues. And a father figure
rises to replace the fading dealer.
Élie Faure. Twenty years the painter's

senior, Faure was a critic's author.
His landmark *History of Art* unveiled
a universalist's account of culture

and the arts where avant-gardists railed
against the grand tradition. A solitary
mind, his unobstructed views were hailed

as purely French. Essays consolatory,
seeing all as one across a screen
of individual illuminations, told the story.

Not surprisingly, he wrote about Soutine:
"Here the holy mystery shines forth.
A flesh more flesh than flesh itself. A stream

of rubies, sulfurous flames, sensations worth
their weight in elemental matter wrung
to vaulting depths of quintessential earth.

Today a lonely heir to Rembrandt paints among
the multitude of manifestoed daubers
in the capital of Western art. A young

man from the Russian shtetl's desperate quarters.
Dare I say it? Here we have a genius."

Soutine fell in love with Faure's daughter.

But not before a deep and inauspicious
friendship bloomed between the critic and
the painter. Only in surviving letters

can we read how the connection spanned
a difference best illustrated by
facility with written French. A grand

divide across the wide Elysian sky
closed over in a shared regard
for absolutes beyond modernity.

Soutine found love and solace in the hard
break from Zborwoski in an afternoon
spent with a kindred soul at the vanguard

of intellectual life in France. And soon,
he would accompany Faure's family to Spain
on a vacation. A photo serves as a cartoon,

a comic window to a closed domain—
Soutine, behind the wheel of Faure's Renault,
is pressed against the young Marie-Zéline,

her father to her right. The critic's son
reflected on the driver's door is shooed,
backhanded, by the driver. Taken from

behind, we see the artist's head, a crude-
cut coif against the girl's enormous hat.
But nothing lasts forever. I allude

to letters. Here, to wit: "Soutine (note that
I do not write 'Monsieur'), your letter lays
no small amount of love and friendship flat.

Please know that no one in my family says
the words you scribble to our attribution.
We have not mocked, cut down, or had our way

with you in your imagined 'parlors.' My position,
I had hoped, was somewhat clearer, friend.
And I frankly do not have the constitution

for your rank ingratitude. *The end*
is how I'd frame things, given your response
to my decision in a letter that was penned

at some expense of heart. You'll see this once
you find yourself, perhaps, a little quieter.
Soutine, you are atrociously unjust.

Signed: Élie Faure." At issue was his daughter.
Kikoïne would tell the story years
after the war in interviews, the water

having passed beneath the bridge, the tears
no longer warm: "He visited my wife
and me. He needed sympathetic ears.

He told us, for the first time in his life,
that he was certain he had found a woman
whom he loved. He told a story rife

with all the disappointment and that omen
of the wandering Jew to which we were acquainted
since our childhood. Apparently the woman

was the daughter of an eminent if not sainted
family in Paris. I will give no names.
She may have been a sitter that he painted.

I believe he knew her father. Just the same,
he told us that he kept his peace for months
and then approached the parents. And his claim

is that the father came around in time. A hunt
for an apartment already under way,
he approached the woman, finally confident

his overture of love would win the day.
He said she listened kindly, then she smiled.
'Soutine, you should have spoken yesterday,'

she said. For just the day before, by wild
coincidence, a cousin asked the girl
to be his wife! An aviator and a child,

Soutine described him. He began to hurl
rude epithets regarding the old man.
I felt sorry for him. No love in the world,

it seemed, for Chaïm. But, then, the master plan
is somewhat shaky. The woman's happiness
was short-lived. Her young husband crashed his plane."

Kikoïne's portrayal of this business
leaves no question—Soutine's break with Faure
was a matter of a doomed proposal and his

no-doubt inappropriate foray
into a world of hurtful accusations,
a surely self-demolishing display.

Faure contributed to publications
of the Popular Front and traveled abroad.
He purchased paintings. There are indications

that a reconciliation would evolve, but toward
the end of 1936 the men
remained estranged. Perhaps some new accord

developed unrecorded. Soutine's pen
expressed his admiration to Faure's
wife the year the writer died. By then

the world was at the brink. What's more,
Soutine's domestic situation was
in flux. The future hung a harrowed door.

*　　　*　　　*

IV

My father died, a suicide at home
when I was 22. The family slept
as Dad did up his knot and dropped the bomb.

It was a Monday morning and it crept
up fast, whatever made him take his life.
I cut the rope, so the detectives kept

me in the kitchen. They were rife
with clumsy questions from an episode
of *Adam-12*. Well, yes. There *was* a knife

involved—their inquiry was up to code.
Adrenalin allowed me ample space
to answer calmly. I did not explode.

I got along, as did my family, in the face
of something that would seem impossible
to handle. Until it happens. There is grace

abundant in the universe. A practical
imperative to get along. To thrive.
As my poet friend, Ray Pospisil,

makes clear, the love of life keeps us alive
until it happens. Until the bell is rung.
I met him two year after Dad's demise.

He was my editor. I'd grabbed the bottom rung,
which had eluded me since graduation.
I looked up to Ray. The guy was young,

and sharp, and talented. My situation
hinged, I thought, on Pospisil's approval.
My first job in New York, a bleak recession—

I had to make it work. "The stark fist of removal,"
Ray would joke when copy hit the bin.
He was "tough but fair." And driven. Robert Duvall

with a smattering of Carl Bernstein in
a newly wired newsroom. Raymond passed
as father figure—I'll admit—within

a friendship. This situation, too, would pass.
When Ray resigned, I was promoted to his pen.
And then the chief resigned. "Well, that was fast,"

said Ray when I got kicked upstairs again.
That conversation proved to be our last
for several years (approximately ten).

In retrospect, a decade blows right past.
And in those years, I traveled to L.A.,
the magazine was virtually trashed

and sold to suits in Philadelphia,
and I began to teach myself to paint.
Maureen—we married in 1984,

the year that I met Ray—had done a stint,
part time, with an artist who ran fairs
at Lincoln Center. Paul. His patron saints

were swordsmen prominent among the heirs
to Rembrandt. He would prep me for the Fauves.
I met him at an exhibition where

his paintings, heavy with ethereal mauves
he'd obviously mixed from cadmiums,
cast Hoboken off-kilter from above

the line of grounded sight. The epithelium
of cracking colors drew me in. In time,
I reached the point of reaching out to him

regarding my ambitions at the easel. "I'm
impressed," he told me when I showed my barges
from the Met. But my palette lacked a rhyme

and meter, a control of color. My corsages
squeezed from tubes, he showed me, paled before
the corresponding hues he mixed, barrages

flying from the primaries into a more
determined wheel of working pigments. "Light,"
he said. "And contrast. And you *must* ignore

the details. Find the forms and set your sight
on gesture, not on line. There are no lines
in nature." The man was absolutely right,

I thought. He set a standard. There are signs
in landscape that require us to see,
to *learn* to see, to read them. Sunlight shines

on objects, but the artist finds the sea
of inner light that shines as a response.
For years I painted, thinking, what would *he*

think. Weingarten was my only audience.
My mentor. I'd show him work infrequently.
We'd talk. We did each other's portraits once.

I painted first, then lunch, and then he painted me.
I fell asleep, which really pissed him off.
He said my painting had some qualities.

By that I knew that he approved. Of course
he checked his praise as any mentor would.
I sold that portrait to his dealer in New York.

I settled in. The job uptown was good,
across the street from the A.S.L. One day
the phone rang. I immediately understood

the import of the call—the voice was Ray's!
Now freelancing, his expertise was energy.
Ol' Pos and I found interesting ways

to work together, and the entropy
in our relationship was thrown into reverse.
In time, we shared another interest. Poetry.

For just as Pospisil recited verse,
especially Lord Tennyson, at work,
he wrote his own. Tremendous stuff, of course.

Book
V

Chapter 1

$\mathcal{G}$arde

I

Gerda Groth met Chaïm at the Café
de Flore on Boulevard Saint-Germain. She'd seen
his work at galleries, where she spent her Saturdays,

and felt a strong affinity for the scenes
and still lifes that he painted. And the portraits.
Gerda lived for pictures, and the reds and greens

that balanced in the turmoil of the tortured
forms he brought to life engaged her soul.
She wouldn't shy from saying so, and told

him when she introduced herself. "Hello.
Monsieur Soutine, I wonder, may I have
a word with you?" Her eyes as black as coal,

looked fervently in Chaïm's. "I've spent half
the afternoon admiring your work. I love
your paintings. I would say, and please don't laugh,

you are the most important painter of
our time." "Madame, would you care to join us here?"
Guillaume inquired as she pulled off a glove.

"Join us, yes!" Soutine sat forward. Gerda, in her
nervousness, smiled broadly, her vampirous eyes—
she cut a dark and awkward figure—shimmered

as she stared at Chaïm, mesmerized.
"Perhaps." She said. She slid her narrow hips
between the café chairs. "I'm not surprised

by your assessment … Madame …" She curled her lips
"It's Groth." She shook the beaming dealer's hand.
"I'm Gerda Groth." Her slender fingertips,

withdrawing from the gentle handshake, fanned
around her elbows as she crossed her arms.
"Monsieur Soutine, I think I understand

what you are trying to convey with form.
I come from Germany, but my family's
from Lithuania. And you are from

that area?" "I went to university
in Vilna, Madame Garde," said Chaïm.
Taken back, she smiled nervously.

"It's Groth," she said. And Chaïm smiled. In time
he would refer to her exclusively
as Mademoiselle Garde, his ardent guardian.

II

Paulette no longer called on Chaïm in Paris.
The fallout with Zborowski broke her heart—
Soutine retreated to the studio, a ferrous

arrogance came over him. For Paulette's part,
concern for Chaïm and her ties to Léopold
confused and paralyzed her. Soutine's art

commanded ever-higher prices. Bold
collectors battled at the auctions, hot
for Cagnes landscapes. Paintings sold

for more than Barnes paid Léo for the lot
in 1923. And soon Krémègne and Kikoïne
pulled back, believing Chaïm's ascendancy was not

reflective of aesthetic values. A keen
artistic jealousy set in among
the Russian corps in Montparnasse. Soutine

was isolated at the top, a rung
or two below Léger and miles below
Picasso. He felt abandoned, and he clung

to the Castaings and Gerda Groth. A show
at Galerie Percier showcased his choirboys,
but Chaïm, again the recluse, did not go.

In the days that followed, new domestic joys,
a love Soutine had never yet experienced,
were cut with chronic pain. If fate deployed

an angel once again, there was a sense
that this time "guardian" was a full-time job.
Mademoiselle Garde came in at the expense

of sharing a creative anguish and the throb
of sleepless episodes that last a week
or more. Lovemaking often ended with a sob,

with charcoal eyes wide open, an antique
depiction of the tragic lover given
to her passion for the hero. Weak,

immortal, wise, already gone, a riven
figure praying in the wake of some Pompeii,
she mothers Chaïm. And in her arms, he is forgiven.

III

The Chartres Cathedral in a patch of sun
lay almost lost against the nimbus clouds
as Chaïm laid down a tarp. He had the run

of a gravel walkway. First he laid the shrouds
of background grays against the board, and then
he brought the structure forward. Sunday crowds

encircled him, but kept their distance. At ten
or so, the light had given way to shadow.
Chaïm kept at it. His palette was a fen

of tertiary greens and grays. A cardinal
passed across the wooden doors. A touch
of cadmium to blood the base. The callow

tones found contrast on the board in much
the same way clouds in layered skies surmount
the drowning wash to build a stairway. Clutch

and lever, lines and folding brushstrokes mount
the brilliant firmament above. Cerulean
space suggests the eye of God, a haunt

of winged legions in their white cotillion.
Weighted to the ground, Soutine looks up
and moves his brushes over the vermilion

chapel rooftops to the spires that crop
above the swaddling of titanium.
The board runs out. The spires do not stop.

He packs his snapping brushes in a scrum
of crumpled tubes rolled in a canvas bag
and folds his easel. Farewell to Elysium—

he throws his kit in Marcellin's car, drives back
to the estate and finds a strip of pine
behind his studio. A hammer crack

or two so that the wood supports align,
and now his board accommodates the fortress
of the Lord. He signs it with his visceral *Soutine*.

Chapter 2

Villa Seurat

I

Youki Desnos smiles when she recalls
Soutine. The poet's wife (Fujita named
her Youki when they lived in Montparnasse)

is sympathetic: "I think he was ashamed
of how his broken French put him across.
But his intellect was obvious. It flamed.

A constant fire. And I was at a loss
when he discussed the literature he read.
He mocked my Proust. I laughed at him because

he read philosophy. 'You fill your head
with Nietzsche? It's beyond belief, Soutine.
So serious!' Of course, it must be said

he worshiped Balzac. He was a cross between
a scholar and a madman. But I thought
him very interesting. Handsome, even."

The Ukrainian sculptor Chana Orloff caught
him at his easel by surprise one day.
His room was utter filth. Villa Seurat

encouraged open studios and doors the way
La Ruche or La Cité Falguière begat
communal space. But Chaïm didn't play

the game. He stayed shut in, "A kind of brat.
I didn't care at all. I came inside
and found him in pajamas and a hat

with scissors, cutting canvas, wild-eyed.
I realized he was tearing up his paintings!
It was violent. A kind of suicide.

At first, I thought I'd caught him masturbating."
Then she saw the pieces that he glued
together on a canvas. "… Fascinating."

Jean Cocteau had less to say. And you'd
have thought that Blaise Cendrars had met
some feral ghost at the Castaings'. *L'étude*

du Juif errant, Soutine would wear his hat
at lunch. Of course he'd come with Gerda Garde.
Marcel to Madeleine: "I miss Paulette."

II

Villa Seurat, behind the Cimetière
du Montparnasse, runs underneath a bank
of picture windows, coursing open air.

Before the war, it ran along a rank
of studio apartments. There Soutine
set up a workplace with the lank,

protective lover he named Garde. Between
severe attacks of nausea, he'd amble out
to paint, his palette folding into green

and gold and gray. He took the train to scout
Auxerre and painted on a windy day.
He spent at least a week alone in Chartres,

establishing his easel in the clay
along a tree-lined avenue that ran
away from town. An echo of Céret,

the poplars twist and tangle in a stand.
A country house is hidden, blood-drop red,
behind the gate of trees. A woman and a man,

suggested in a knot of brushstrokes, head
out to the suburbs on the avenue,
an amber wash beneath a verdant spread.

They anchor thunder in the leaves. The two,
the holy standard of *The Jewish Bride*,
abroad beneath the windstorm. *Bienvenue!*

When he came home, the beaming Gerda had
his studio prepared. She welcomed him
with chicken broth and black bread on the side.

III
Anais Nin lived down the hall, among
the luminaries in Chanel and Harris
Tweed. Fedora wearers, old and young.

The ultimate American in Paris,
Henry Miller, penned his famous books
upstairs from Chaïm in Villa Seurat. There is

mention in his *Tropics* of the pastry cooks
in battered arrondissements—they had a few
motifs in common. Miller liked the looks

of Soutine's studio. "He was a Jew.
An Old World Jew, the kind I've always known.
And you can see it in his paintings." Miller knew

primordial expressiveness when shown.
"The angel is my watermark," he wrote
of watercolors. He had done his own.

He painted them from memory. "I noted
the outsider's passion in his art.
The dread, the longing. I came on a boat

myself!" He invited Chaïm to his apart-
ment where he'd set a ping-pong table up.
"We had some models there that night. That sort

of thing. Soutine was rather suave! On top
of Ping-Pong, certainly—he cleaned my clock!
Some German blonde let her kimono drop,

a friend of Max's. Soutine tried to talk
to her—they couldn't find a language. What
the hell. He stammered something through that awk-

ward smile. The two of us were smiling a lot
before the night was through. I liked the guy.
Well, everybody thought he was a nut,

and that was true—but the *artistic* kind.
The kind of nut with heart and fortitude.
He made a lot of noise downstairs. I didn't mind."

And Soutine saw a model that he knew
at Miller's place. He didn't speak with her.
Six years before, she'd posed for Soutine nude.

IV

She was a Russian dancer when they met,
employed at Bersolys on Rue de Lille,
a small hotel. Tatyana hadn't yet

done any modeling. She was eager. Still,
when Soutine fell on her, she'd no idea
about the etiquette. An act of will

on Soutine's part prevailed. "Stand over there,"
he said, positioning a desk lamp with a red
cloth draped across the shade. "Forget your hair.

It's fine." "You want me standing? Should I get
undressed?" He answered yes, and yes, and posed
her, slightly turned, positioning her head

off-center at the upper canvas edge. She closed
her eyes. "No, open them. Stay focused on
the painting over there." Soutine composed

the figure as his model looked upon
a side of beef. Her eyes were opened wide.
The artist stirred his cadmiums around

and started on her face, which looked aside,
perhaps a nod to Orthodox taboo,
but more an echo of *The Jewish Bride*.

Beneath her blushing cheek, an abstract flow
of pink and yellow sagged against the brown-
on-black. Soutine worked rosy colors through

the details of the face. The nose. The swollen
lips, which hit the high red tone that pulls
the eye toward the center of the storm

in Soutine's paintings. Moving to the shoals
of fleshtone underneath, he modeled breasts.
The model quivered nervously. Her folded

hands beneath her soft décolletage
squeezed red on white, the blushing hues
of cheek and ear. And to the nipples, next,

he laid an ochre red. A sweep of blue
along the lower contours of a languid
arm, and then he worked the highlights through

the image in a wave of white as sanguine
flesh, still raw, began to take on weight.
He whited out the nipple on the sagging

breast below the armpit on the right,
which drew attention to the irritated
nipple on the left. A touch of white

as highlight and a shadow compensated
for the overkill. And so, the face,
the hands, a breast. An understatement

carried over to a wordless space,
a feeling rising like the eyebrows over
tired and astonished eyes. Its grace

came forward, and the nude connected to that other
painting of a woman fully clothed. If not
The Jewish Bride, perhaps *The Russian Lover*

with the jaundice yellow belly, taught
and gently rounded, ready to be torn
apart. We have the human body caught

between the temple and the abattoir.
The woman and the hanging side of beef.
There was no pillowed mattress on the floor.

The session ended. Soutine made a brief
distracted bow and paid his Russian model.
He called a cab. And much to her relief,

Tatyana left the artist's cluttered hovel,
twenty francs ahead and unmolested
by this flea-bit painter from the shtetl.

　　　If Modigliani, master of the nude, invested
canvases with sweeps of feminine
repose and flesh, his mastery's contested

by his Russian protégé. Paul Weingarten
describes the Soutine nude as the most grand
portrayal of the human form between

Courbet and, well, whoever's next—a stand
quite gutsy, given all the nakedness
of modern and postmodern art. To understand

his meaning, one looks backward from the mess
to Titian and to Veronese. To Rembrandt.
To Soutine. I like that kind of gutsiness.

V

His ulcer kept the painter from his easel
as the Germans rattled sabers. Garde
monitored both situations, knowing either,

especially the latter, could land hard
or deadly in the space she'd finally found.
According to her immigration card,

she was a German divorcée. Around
the star of David on a seal there ran
a stamp that laid her family history down,

the designation, *Juif.* There'd been a plan
among collectors at the Club des Arts,
a gallery in Chicago that had shown Soutine,

to bring him to America. It fell apart.
"I cannot come—you haven't any trees,"
his odd but adamant reply the start

of something like the end. For three
months he refused to paint. The Castaings
intervened at last and took him to Civry.

He undertook a series on the lanes
of plane trees and another at the farms—
domestic animals. Alive. The spring

of 1940 found the painter's arms
around a mule. The Castaings' new assignment:
gaining Soutine's access to the barns.

His attitude precipitates a climate
of resentment. "Chaïm, this is my *wife*
you're talking to." "*I need the white one, dammit!*"

"We'll get the horse," said Madeleine. "His life
apparently depends upon it." So
it seemed. At dawn, the Castaings trundled off

and came back after lunch. They had a pony
and the farmer's son and kept them over-
night. Soutine apparently destroyed the only

painting of this model. Pigs in clover,
curled together sleeping, made the cut.
Bedraggled cows. Soutine, the donkey lover,

found some peace in living still life, but
began to fall apart with Madeleine.
"Soutine, your timing's off. There are a lot

of, well … considerations. There's a war!
And frankly we're not wild about the pigs,"
she said. "You came at us this way before.

At la Rotonde …" "But I don't give two figs
for ancient history," he growled. "And don't
think I don't know my situation. Rags

and bones. A Jew in France. Madame, I want
you to *support this series*. Pulling out
the minute I change course! Come on! I can't

believe it!" Madeleine stood firm. "Well, count
me as a former painter in your stable."
He grabbed the canvas and he said goodnight.

"Soutine, I'd buy it now if I were able.
We've cut back entirely, and …" "*Fine*,"
he shrieked. He left her at the kitchen table.

And the wind gust that he left in turned to rain.
He trudged along the dark streets of Civry.
He would not make the Monday morning train

to Paris. Madeleine would mark the day
he walked into the windstorm as the fall
of night. A blackout. A catastrophe.

Chapter 3

Soutine in the Wind

I

A dream of ashen clouds on hurling oaks.
A rolling darkness. Children wander lost.
A ragged cut of sky that lingers chokes

on burnt sienna. Borders have been crossed.
The mayor of Civry informs Soutine
that he must keep from Paris at all costs,

that Gerda Groth, who stayed behind, was seen
among the immigrants detained at Gurs,
a camp for "foreign Jews" in Aquitaine.

A dream of being rolled into a hearse
departing Paris in the morning rain.
A dream, and not a dream. And rolling in reverse ....

II

Another lover comes awake and slowly
rises from a simple iron bed.
She swoons, as if she feels the room is rolling.

Dropping in a chair she holds her head,
her fingers clenched and tugging at her hair.
She stands again and grabs a bottle bled

entirely the night before, despair
and pain, confusion in her eyes, her satin
nightgown torn and stained. "Where is it? Where ..."

165

She strains her eyes, and then her body slackens
as she grabs a second bottle, falling back.
All hell is manageable once it happens.

"Soutine," she stammers. With a smoker's hack
she fumbles for a broken cigarette.
The painter, curled into a cul-de-sac

beneath the covers, moans. "We're not there yet,
Soutine. We have to leave. C'mon. Get up."
She stands again. "There's still a little anisette."

III

A dream and not a dream. A bleeding life.
A canvas on which subtle forms are drifting.
Mother, nurse, a model or a wife,

the lines and their relationship keep shifting.
One loses track of time. Our sense of place
is the illusion of a curtain lifting ....

        Marcellin finds her in Gare Montparnasse,
disoriented, standing in the grim
queue waiting for the next train to Alsace.

He grabs her shoulder and she turns to him.
"Monsieur Castaing!" She trembles, nearly faints.
"Thank God," he whispers to the seraphim

of grime and to the gritty station saints
receding in the architecture. "Come
with me." He walks her slowly from the trains

and to his car. "I'm going to take you home,"
where Madeleine is pacing nervously,
before a student copy of Gérôme's

Pygmalion in her parlor. Under three
Soutine's—a country house, a pheasant and
her portrait. On an antique desk we see

a photograph—Zborowksi and Soutine
together at the races, done up to the nines.
Finally, she hears them. "Madeleine!"…

        Summer burned as Germany redrew the lines.
The camp at Gurs, reshuffled to the Free Zone,
let female detainees who could provide

a proof of residence return. The season
burned. And Gerda Groth got on the train
to Paris. Beyond all hope, beyond all reason

she had written Madelaine ....

                "Soutine,"
cried Gerda as she and Marcellin tumbled through
the parlor door. "Tell me, have you heard from Chaïm?"

Her benefactor sighed. "Ah, Mademoiselle.
I am so glad to see you." Marcellin frowned
and shook his head, quite clearly overwhelmed.

"Tell me, Madame. Tell me, have you found
Soutine?" It proved impossible to stanch
the woman's sharp anxiety. She'd ground

Marcellin, who pleaded ignorance, to hunched
and nervous silence at the wheel. The Castaings
knew about Marie-Berthe Aurenche,

Max Ernst's former wife, who'd taken Chaïm
beneath her wing in recent months. That news
struck Madeleine as very sad and strange.

This doyenne of the Dadaists was bent
on keeping Soutine from his friends and out
of Vichy hands. The Castaings heard they went

to Champigny-sur-Veude and there, no doubt,
the woman, known to be delusional,
and Chaïm had fashioned some arcane redoubt

of codependency. The usual
arrangement for Soutine. Had Gerda not
been Chaïm's protector once? And up until

their fallout, did she herself not hold the spot
of mother figure for this falling man?
This homeless child? And here was Gerda Groth ....

"Just tell me what you know, Monsieur Castaing.
Madame? They've not detained him at a camp.
Oh, *tell* me that." Madeleine took her hand,

and looking up, she caught her husband's glance.
She understood and she agreed. "No, Gerda."
She told her what she knew of Chaïm's circumstance.

IV

"Another reason to leave France," says Max
as Marie-Berthe leaves the dining room.
This time she didn't throw the plates. In fact

she spoke politely to Leonora Carrington,
her replacement at the family table.
"My blessings on you both. What's done is done,"

she said. And Jimmy, Max's son, was able
to express his love before all present.
He kissed the woman's cheek. And there the fable

ends. The mystery begins. The latent
story. Marie-Berthe may have met
Soutine at Miller's studio apartment.

She favored the cerebral arts, and yet
the source has undeniable appeal.
She may have come to him the way that Gerda

followed from the galleries. Surreal
gives way to the essential and a downward
swipe, a tearing gesture as a wheel

of fire is set in motion. An absurd
relationship evolves between Soutine
and this delicate French-Catholic bird,

this European ingénue. The dream
proceeds in flashing scenes, in fits and starts.
In blood and alcohol and gasoline.

V

Red wine. It's shadow is the first sensation
bleeding through the rain-gray light on a packet
of Gauloises, in the air of dissipation.

Marie-Berthe, sensing Chaïm can take it,
swings her leg around and takes her waking
lover. Above the knot of sheets, her naked

shoulders roll and tremble to the slaking
trawl, the heaviness of morning love.
This time there's no complaint about an aching

stomach. Marie-Berthe rides above
the painter as he nuzzles at her breasts.
Surprisingly, his slow reaction proves

sufficient. Marie-Berthe lays her fists
into the pillows, bearing down until she comes,
collapsing lifeless on her lover's chest.

She breathes. "You're well today, a blessing from
the Lord." Soutine smiles wanly, "You're confused."
She lifts her head. "Confused, you say. How come?"

"The Lord has bigger eggs to scramble, and the Jews
apparently don't count. I think we slipped
one by him here, my Catholic friend." "I choose

to thank the Lord for every happiness."
"Then you are happy here? With me?" She smiles
and drops her head back on the pillow. "Yes.

And will you paint today?" "I think I will."
She curls into the sheets again and falls
asleep, but only for a little while.

Awakened by a slamming in the hall,
she notices Soutine is not in bed.
She finds her robe but hesitates to call

his name. She listens quietly instead
to intermittent thumps and tearing canvas
as she holds her fists against her head.

Outside the bedroom door, Soutine, half-dressed,
is cutting up a still-wet portrait, smearing
oil paint on carpeting and walls. Countless

jagged gashes rip through the endearing
smile of Marie-Berthe as she locks
herself inside the bedroom, fearing

Chaïm's fury. But when he gently knocks
an hour later, she lets him in the door.
She stands aside. He trundles in and looks

intently at her hands, and then the floor.
"Do *not* correct my paintings. Understand?"
"But the mouth required a little more ..."

He grabs the shaking woman by her hand
and pulls her to the bed. She kisses wildly,
long, encouraging the reprimand.

VI

For weeks on end, he feels quite ill and faint.
He stays in bed with his addictive nurse.
On better days, he goes outside to paint.

He must have read about the change at Gurs.
He must have thought about his lover, Garde.
Two years had passed, and he believes the curse

is irreversible. She has a card
like his. That yellow star is like a scarlet
letter. And she is lost in that regard.

The greens and blues take over Chaïm's palette.
The landscape carries forth a gust of wind
that brushes at the tree line with a mallet.

And the blood begins. Soutine is thin
and sickly. The painter is in constant pain
as mystery evolves toward myth. He's pinned

beneath a sky portending heavy rain
or rolling in a cleansing stream of air.
A pair of children populates the lanes,

a child sprawls beside a pond. A lair
of the abandoned and a bed of firewood
where lolling children lie with tangled hair,

this dream of running home beneath a cloud
gives way to visions of a farm girl at the gate
or at the Dutch doors of a barn. A shroud

of ducklings mimicking their mother's gait
folds feather-green and -blue along the ground.
A run of paintings that anticipate

the end, in open fields that emulate the sound
of thunder, looks backward to the earthquake in Céret.
The spiritual and physical are bound

by gravity sufficient to the day.
A pendent flank, a nightmare dangling.
Cut the rope. The body falls away.

VII

"We're not there yet, Soutine. We have to leave.
C'mon. Get up." No use. She sees that he
is bleeding from his mouth. She grabs her sleeve

and wipes it with a shaking hand. "Soutine!"
She goes out in the hall and grabs two neighbors
who assist in lifting him. Between

the two of them, they get him to the hearse
that Marie-Berthe borrowed as a means
of driving through the checkpoints into Paris

undetected by municipal police.
Soutine requires surgery. The ulcer
has progressed to the point where a disease

of the intestine brings him ever closer
to an incapacity that cannot be reversed.
And the blood keeps rising like a gusher

in his stomach. The drinking made it worse,
of course, as did Marie-Berthe's indecision
and confusion. They'd driven in the hearse

through country mud and forest on a mission,
gathering his paintings from collectors
leaving France. From galleries. Revision

happened. And destruction. His benefactors
gave him canvases to carry off,
entrusted to the *Interdit Secours*.

They piled the pictures in the car, made love
unless his stomach pain was a distraction.
The two were drinking up until he coughed

the morning blood.

                    ~Modigliani's candle
gutters, but the room is somehow bathed
in light and in the atmosphere of scandal

that enshrouds the proud Italian. Scathed
by his immodest habits and consumptive
malady, he leans toward a panel paved

in mauve and gold on which he's scraping something.
Painting by redaction, he exhumes
his portrait of Soutine. And now his haunted

eyes turn slowly to the dreamer. Rooms
shine amber light into a hallway over
Modi's shoulder and a cannon booms

from somewhere in the city. "You will recover,
Chaïm. And you mustn't be afraid.
Be still. And never ask about the other

child again. Or Léopold. He's paid.
We've settled everything. I'm almost finished."
His pentiment is curdled and decayed

in fetid swaths about his boots. The brandished
palette knife cuts skin from cracking panels
to a space through which the portrait's vanished.

It is gone. Modigliani's flannels
vanish. The sparrow and its broken shadow
cross the hall outside. The shadow channels

all to bloody darkness and a shallow
pulse. *Regina Angelorum*. To a vision
bathed in red~

A traffic jam. The callow

driver nods. There is a slight collision
on the rainy road that causes a delay.
There is a far-too-long-delayed incision.

Marie-Berthe watches as they gurney him away,
aware that Soutine will not be revived
again. Marie-Berthe disappears that day

into the Paris wind, unhinged, deprived
of all connection with the world, her love
extinguished with her story. She survives.

VIII

"As I recall, the sky was crystal blue,
and there were summer flowers on the grass
and at the gate they carried Chaïm through.

We buried him in Cimetière du Montparnasse.
I recognized Picasso with Krémègne
and Kikoïne. The look on Madame Castaing's face

I'll not forget. His passing left a stain
of sorrow in her noble eyes, a hard
and steady darkness. We are changed.

Of course, the world was being torn apart.
He was the only man I truly loved." ~

Les souvenirs de Mademoiselle Garde

Epilogue

The Last Supper
(On comparing canvases with Paul Weingarten)

Andrey saw it on my basement easel
in the week before he left. "Holy shit!
The Da Vinci Code!" he said. "Of course, I'm pleased to

see myself as the apostle with
the divot in his hand." I hadn't thought
of that, yet there was Andrey with his thick

red lips and Russian beard, stigmata-hot
alizarin on a palm held just above
the head of Christ. A tragic gesture caught

behind the twelve at table. It would prove
the subject of a poem I'd later write
on reconciliation—Christ the dove

with Christ the firebrand, a setting-right
of things with Paul (a blind collaboration).

My Savior, throwing ectoplasmic light,

glows green amidst a tight-packed congregation.
Seven hands are shown in several states
of prayer, embrace, or wild gesticulation.

Christ points upward as he contemplates
the hour to come. His hour is the hardest,
but he's surrounded by a dozen fates

less clear. The Bonaparte and Bonapartist
under Roman rule—conventional, which might
explain its provenance: Destroyed by artist.

Weingarten's Christ is more the acolyte
to His disciples, who are European
Jews. Hasidim. Jesus, dressed in white,

seats John and Judas. Peter, James and Simon
have the porkpie hats or kaftans. Others
wearing robes seem more like fishermen.

An *Internationale*. A band of brothers,
seated, each, before a dinner roll,
uneasy. A trinity of death masks hovers

on the shoulders of the Christ. Behold
the nontraditional!
                    I meld the two
interpretations in my poem, and I'm told

that it's accepted in the next *Shit Creek Review!*
I've kept a color print of mine. But Paul's
is sold, unphotographed. They'll need his too,

so I agree to pay a Sunday call
to the collector with my camera.
The painting's hanging on an old brick wall

in a solarium, the cafeteria
of a retirement home for Catholic priests,
radical Jesuits and intellectuals,

beside an ancient gym on Thompson Street
in SoHo—Father Daniel Berrigan
among them. But the priest that I will meet

is Father Joseph Towle. A gentle man,
quite small and frail, but lively. Rather trusting,
as he leads me, in his snow-white cardigan,

to where the painting hangs beside a rusting
pot of laurentii and coleus. "How's the light?"
"It's perfect." I take little time adjusting

the mechanics—cut the flash. The man in white
has left me to my task, and I shoot a dozen
pictures. "It's going to be cool tonight,"

the Father says, returning. "Ah but doesn't
that portrayal of the supper tell it all?
We're very proud to own it. It says something

utterly unique and true." "Yes. Paul
does splendid work." "You know, it's very Jewish.
Eastern European. The hats, the shawl.

And just the faces." "And it's Jesus who is
serving them." "He brings them all together.
He loves them very much. This painting's true as

Leonardo's, isn't it? It offers up *another*
view. It makes us feel the sacrifice. The love."
Our conversation turns again to weather

as he shows me out. We pass a picture of
the crucifixion—"Another of your friend's."

Near falling into layered clouds above
our heads, the Christian archetype transcends
mere Christianity beside a doorway open
to a neighborhood that never ends.

The End

AFTERWORD

One of the advantages poetry has in telling a story is its cinematographic quality—its reliance on imagery and a creative interpretation of events. Meetings and dialogue included in *Soutine* are created on the basis of biographical sources such as those listed below. While I have accorded myself a great deal of what might be called, in the best sense, poetic license, few scenes are entirely imagined, and these tend to take place in bedrooms. The book is finally my depiction of the artist's experience as I interpret and intuit it from his work and from the small spread of biographical sketches available in English, from letters, and from photographs. In essence, I present my experience of Soutine.

Books and other sources I have consulted in my research include the *Soutine: Catalogue Raisonné* published by Taschen; *Modigliani: The Biography*, by William Fifield; *Chaïm Soutine*, published by Prestel as a catalog for the retrospective of Soutine's work that traveled to The Jewish Museum in New York, the Los Angeles County Museum of Art, and the Cincinnati Art Museum in 1998 and 1999; *About Modern Art, Critical Essays 1948-1997* by David Sylvester; and *Chaïm Soutine*, a monograph published by Harry N. Abrams with text by Alfred Werner. The documentary film *Soutine the Obsessed*, part of a series titled *Montparnasse Revisited* issued in VHS format by Homevision in 2000, was extremely informative, as were my discussions with painters who know and love Soutine's work, in particular my discussions with Paul Weingarten.

I hope the reader of *Soutine* will also have a book of his paintings at hand as a reference. The Taschen catalogue raisonné, with essays by Maurice Tuchman, Esti Dunow, and Klaus Perls, is the most comprehensive.

Rick Mullin
October 31, 2011

183

Other Books from Dos Madres Press

Michael Autrey - *From The Genre Of Silence* (2008)
Paul Bray - *Things Past and Things to Come* (2006), *Terrible Woods* (2008)
Jon Curley - *New Shadows* (2009)
Deborah Diemont - *The Wanderer* (2009)
Joseph Donahue - *The Copper Scroll* (2007)
Annie Finch - *Home Birth* (2004)
Norman Finkelstein - *An Assembly* (2004), *Scribe* (2009)
Gerry Grubbs - *Still Life* (2005), *Girls in Bright Dresses Dancing* (2010)
Richard Hague - *Burst, Poems Quickly* (2004)
Pauletta Hansel - *First Person* (2007), *What I Did There* (2011)
Michael Heller - *A Look at the Door with the Hinges Off* (2006),
    Earth and Cave (2006)
Michael Henson - *The Tao of Longing & The Body Geographic* (2010)
Eric Hoffman - *Life At Braintree* (2008), *The American Eye* (2011)
James Hogan - *Rue St. Jacques* (2005)
Keith Holyoak - *My Minotaur* (2010)
David M. Katz - *Claims of Home* (2011)
Burt Kimmelman - *There Are Words* (2007), *The Way We Live* (2011)
Richard Luftig - *Off The Map* (2006)
J. Morris - *The Musician, Approaching Sleep* (2006)
Robert Murphy - *Not For You Alone* (2004), *Life in the Ordovician* (2007)
Peter O'Leary - *A Mystical Theology of the Limbic Fissure* (2005)
Bea Opengart - *In The Land* (2011)
David A. Petreman - *Candlelight in Quintero - bilingual edition* (2011)
Paul Pines - *Reflections in a Smoking Mirror* (2011)
David Schloss - *Behind the Eyes* (2005)
William Schickel - *What A Woman* (2007)
Murray Shugars - *Songs My Mother Never Taught Me* (2011)
Nathan Swartzendruber - *Opaque Projectionist* (2009)
Jean Syed - *Sonnets* (2009)
Madeline Tiger - *The Atheist's Prayer* (2010), *From The Viewing Stand* (2011)
James Tolan - *Red Walls* (2011)
Henry Weinfield - *The Tears of the Muses* (2005),
    Without Mythologies (2008), *A Wandering Aramaean* (2012)
Donald Wellman - *A North Atlantic Wall* (2010)
Tyrone Williams - *Futures, Elections* (2004), *Adventures of Pi* (2011)
Martin Willitts Jr. - *Secrets No One Must Tell* (2011)

www.dosmadres.com